# simply JESUS

Byron McWilliams

CROSSBOOKS
PUBLISHING

CrossBooks™
A Division of LifeWay
1663 Liberty Drive
Bloomington, IN 47403
www.crossbooks.com
Phone: 1-866-879-0502

First published by CrossBooks 12/12/2013

ISBN: 978-1-4627-3234-0 (sc)
ISBN: 978-1-4627-3236-4 (hc)
ISBN: 978-1-4627-3235-7 (e)

Library of Congress Control Number: 2013922103

Printed in the United States of America.

This book is printed on acid-free paper.

Any people depicted in stock imagery provided by Thinkstock are models,
and such images are being used for illustrative purposes only.
Certain stock imagery © Thinkstock.

With an overflowing heart of gratitude for making this book become more than a dream, I say a very special thank you to my dear friend…

Joyce Fisher

This book is dedicated to my wonderful wife and partner in ministry. I could not do what I do if not for her wisdom, prayers, encouragement and love! I love you Andi (BATW)!

# contents

"For the earth will be filled with the knowledge of the glory of the LORD as the waters cover the sea."

Habakkuk 2:14

# chapter 1
## A BUBBLE OF OUR OWN DESIGN

WHETHER WE LIKE IT OR not, we are rut-oriented people. Of course, we deny this when someone says that a rut is just a grave with the ends kicked out. With feigned laughter we quickly reject our affinity for the rut-driven lifestyle, while in all truthfulness, we know ourselves too well. So for the next few sentences, I'm going to pick on the American male, but ladies, I don't want you to gain an idea that this book is just for men. As a woman, you face an equally strong pull toward living in a rut. The analogy I'm using crosses gender lines, and I think you'll get the message, too.

Apart from a few daring, perhaps foolish souls who wear Red Bull on their jerseys, American men settle for the ease of comfort over the rush of adrenaline. As manly men, we like a taste of excitement and challenge but not enough to get too extreme. We get our kicks from watching the X-Games, our favorite college football team or ESPN's Top Ten on TV while sitting in our La-Z-Boy recliners living the dream. (As I write this I'm reminding myself that my large brown chair is called a La-Z-Boy for a reason!) The older we get the less we crave excitement, the less the adrenaline flows. We quietly become enveloped in a bubble of our own design.

As independent-minded souls, we choose what we want to watch on television and read only the books that entertain and capture our interest. We usually get our news from FOX or CNN, rarely from both. We complain about politics, realizing that while we will never be world changers in this arena we can still express our opinion. As we age, our list of friends shrinks and narrows. We justify this by telling ourselves that the simple life is what is most important.

If we are like a growing percentage of American males, we rarely go to church on Sunday. It's our only day, so we say, to catch up on a little extra sleep and do those "honey do's" that always hover just below the surface. We make excuses for not dating our wife and then wonder why she's less prone to say "yes" than she is to clean the toilet. Involvement with our kid's lives is more on a "have to" basis rather than "want to" because the office, tee time, or something equally as important demands our immediate attention. We have developed a bubble of our own design that controls our lives, but by no means are we stuck in a rut.

At certain times, we may pause to reflect our lives seem to be missing something, but it's hard to put a finger on what it may be. We have been desensitized with our bubble life and cannot smell the strong odor of excessive comfort wafting about.

If we work in an office, we experience this even more than men who actually use their hands and strong backs for a living. Our desk job muscles grow soft and we become thicker around the middle. We forget that God created us as the protectors of our families. We were designed by our Creator to be a hunter, one who kills so those living closest to us in our cave or tent can eat. There is little of this today. Besides, we have an alarm system to handle safety needs and a supermarket to buy our meat. By the time we have reached middle age, the bubble we float through life in has become so well-padded that we have all but forgotten our purpose as men, as Christian men.

A typical day of the week may go like this: We arise to meet the day from our comfortable bed where we've just received 6-8 hours of sleep on padded mattresses that cost more than our first car. We struggle to get up because we've been in the womb of a warm comforter all night as we've enjoyed our perfectly controlled 71-degree sleep experience. We make our way into a comfortably hot shower and then dry off with soft, comfortable lavender scented towels. We put on comfortable clothing that doesn't make us itch. Before we head out the door, we make our way to our coffee maker for the convenience of a comfortably warm cup of coffee. We then get into our oh-so comfortable sedan, possibly a pickup truck, but only if it has the proper amenities, and we embark on our morning drive to our comfortable office. Are you beginning to see a pattern here?

We exert our energies for four hours in mid-level meetings and planning sessions before heading off to lunch with several friends whom we're comfortable with from the office. After arriving back in the office, we attempt to work but the comfort of the office chair combined with a delightfully full stomach severely limits our productivity and we'd much rather take a comfortable nap instead. Somehow we make it through our less than productive afternoon before heading home for the day.

Upon arrival, we meet others of our clan to enjoy a comfortable evening together. We eat our comfort food before settling into our most comfortable chair to be soothed by our favorite television shows. At the appropriate time and after having eaten a comforting snack, we put the dogs out, turn out the lights and snuggle back into our comfortable bed only to repeat the experience the next day. We have just enjoyed another day of adventurous living in the bubble of our own design.

Have I made my redundant point? Is it any wonder why American men are bored with life? Could this be the reason so many seek to introduce excitement into their life through extra-marital affairs, overdone hobbies, extreme workaholic tendencies, or some other self-prescribed distraction? We are bored with the bubbles we've created and we don't know how to recapture the excitement we once had about living. The rut is killing us and we want to break free, but we have no idea how. We want something rugged so that the emasculated feelings we get from a lack of adrenaline can be countered with an "I've still got it!" proclamation as we point to the "S" on our chest.

This was driven home to me recently when my wife and I watched *The Ghost and Mrs. Muir.* It's an old black-and-white film about a handsome sea captain who haunts his old house where the beautiful widow, Mrs. Muir, resides. As the story unfolds, they enjoy each other's company and become fast friends. When Mrs. Muir runs into financial trouble, the salty old sailor dictates his life story to her. He knows it will sell, providing Mrs. Muir a much needed income so she will not have to move.

When Mrs. Muir takes the book to the publisher and he reluctantly agrees to give it a brief glance, my point is made. The publisher expected another boring romance novel written from a love deprived woman. What he found was the swashbuckling account of a rugged man's life on the high seas sailing from seaport to seaport and encountering one adventure after another. The middle-aged publisher was so taken by the sea captain's exciting life that he spent the next several hours reading the book in one sitting. His imagination and dreams were stirred as he was taken captive by the bold adventures that he longed for but knew he would never have. While God created men for bold adventures, most today would have to admit they are much more the middle-aged book publisher than the salty sea-captain.

Where has the adventure of living gone? Who stole your adrenaline rush?

## Jesus and Bubbles

Jesus never hesitated to pop the bubbles of those who crossed His path. He called both men and women out of their comfort zone to come follow Him. He also popped the bubbles of religious leaders determined to ensnare Him with their lies and foolish tests. Jesus was always a step ahead of the opposition because He was as wise as a serpent and as gentle as a dove.[1]

When Jesus crossed paths with the first century Galilean society, He saw crowds of people suffering the ravages of living in a fallen world. In almost every way that matters, the people were no different than us living in the twenty-first century. The same troubles faced years ago are the same many face every morning today. Illness, financial woes, relationship disasters and death were just as common 2,000 years ago as they are today. Let's not romanticize the past to the point that it is no longer biblically accurate.

To some it would have been prudent for Jesus to look at those he met and provide philosophical reasons for their struggles, telling them to "hang in there!" He did no such thing. Some imagine Jesus being a sort of first century "Dr. Phil" to help people identify what was and was not working for them so they could fix all their problems and be happy. Jesus did nothing of the sort. His tactics for helping others were not derived from a dependent culture in need of a quick fix. Instead, Jesus traveled from village, town, synagogue and market popping bubbles as He called people to higher levels of spiritual accountability than ever dreamed.

He popped the bubbles of His early disciples, knowing that the Gospel would not advance apart from ready participants willing to live bubble-free lives. With divinely spoken words, Jesus painted an adventurous picture for those He summoned to spread His Gospel message. He didn't hesitate to ask a fisherman to drop his net, make a life-changing career move, and come

---

1   See Matthew chapter 10 for the full context. All Scripture references are from the English Standard Version translation unless otherwise denoted.

follow Him. When He looked at the woman at the well, Jesus did not shrink from telling her insights into her life only God could know so that she would become an instrument to announce the Messiah. As Jesus walked under a fig tree and saw a small man named Zacchaeus, without embarrassment Jesus called him from his comfort zone as a tax collector to a life of adventure with Him. Jesus delights when those who confess Him as Lord give evidence of His lordship by answering the Gospel's call to action.

These are biblical examples of Jesus popping bubbles. My contention is that He operates no differently today when He encounters a life in need of change than He did when he walked dusty trails between villages. While we cannot see Him visually, the call to drop the net, come down from the tree, or go tell a family member to "come and see" is just as powerful. Jesus masterfully wrecks our comfort zones because he refuses to soft-pedal His demands for bubble living people. He knows that comfort zones steal the cutting edge from our lives and dull our senses and emotions and He not only wants more from us, He wants more for us.

In the Great Commission, Jesus commands His followers to live their lives outside the bubble of their own design. Matthew 28:19-20 records His words, "Go therefore and make disciples of all nations, baptizing them in the name of the Father and of the Son and of the Holy Spirit, teaching them to observe all that I have commanded you. And behold, I am with you always, to the end of the age." This has action-oriented and adventurous living contained in every syllable. Look at the words the Lord uses: go, make, baptize, and teach. Why are we to do this? The short answer is that we have been commanded by Jesus. What are we to do? We are to proclaim and teach the Gospel in our areas of influence because the world is full of people who need to hear what God has in store for them. The Gospel transcends all socio-economic, racial, geographic and political boundaries. It pierces the darkness with divine light and reveals truth amid lies.

The Gospel is the call of God to enter into a life of warfare as real as the RPG's and small weapons fire faced by our soldiers in Afghanistan. It is the command of our Lord to confront with His truth the mushrooming lostness found in the more than seven billion people on earth. When the bubble is popped, we are suddenly awakened to a world filled with the global threat of Al Qaeda terrorism, religious extremism, smart bombs, racial hatred, substance abuse, pornography, gender confusion, sex trafficking and rampant political correctness. None of which will be resolved through education, military action or pie-in-the-sky prayers for peaceful coexistence. The only strategy guaranteed to bring success was given by God and is found in the Bible. His guarantee is the Gospel of Jesus Christ. When we embrace the call to share the Gospel with others, we find a swashbuckling and thrilling life awaiting us. A life filled with adrenaline that far surpasses the excitement of Red Bull extreme sports. God's call to participate with him in the Gospel is His invitation to embrace a life of eternal significance. To do so, however, we must rise from our La-Z-Boys and fully engage!

## "Let's live the adventure!"

I will never forget one particular Sunday, Andi and I sat in church listening to our pastor preach the Gospel. For the past 8 years we had been part of an incredible faith community in Northwest Houston known as Champion Forest Baptist Church. The life of comfort we had embraced included friends from church, a solid career for me as an accountant for a major oil company and Andi being blessed to stay at home with our family as we watched it grow one precious baby at a time. But it was all about to change!

By this time in our lives, we were no different than every friend we had; upward mobility was the name of the game. Andi and I were in our early thirties. We had two children and a third on the way. Our next move up the social ladder had been discussed and we were picking the neighborhood school we wanted our kids to attend. Life for the McWilliams' family was good and getting better.

I was a volunteer bible teacher for young adults on Sunday mornings while Andi was a student of Precept Bible studies. We were theologically grounded and took seriously the will of God. And for us, that's when it happened.

I began experiencing "feelings" like I'd never known. If you and I met, you would probably arrive at a conclusion sooner than later that I am not a man tossed about by my feelings. I like the grounded approach for living. One of my catch phrases is "What's the game plan?" I believe in practical living with both feet on the ground. I'm a fixer, just ask my wife. Give me a plan and I'm set. If it's truth, I'm drawn to it. If it's subjective and full of gray areas, I tend to set that aside. I'm a "just the facts ma'am" kind of guy like Sargent Joe Friday on the old *Dragnet* series. But for some reason, I was unable to shake the feeling that something was not right spiritually. It didn't matter what my pastor was preaching, the growing sense that Jesus was asking me for additional surrender would not go away. God was relentlessly pursuing me, calling me to release my grip on the dreams and plans I'd developed and deemed so important.

When I shared this with Andi she was receptive to whatever God might be doing. Her encouragement was to ride this out and see it through. When I was tempted to throw in the towel and tell her it was nothing, she was quick to help me refocus and persevere. I think she was as interested as I in what God was up to. So we prayed together, read our Bibles and talked late into the night about life.

On one particular day, I had set a meeting to go visit with my pastor about what I had been experiencing. It was one of those days when nothing seemed to go right at work and I had decided to call the church and cancel my meeting. When I told Andi my plan she shot my idea of canceling down and told me the work would be there tomorrow, just "Go!" It was the kind of great advice I had learned to expect from my wife.

When I arrived at my pastor's office and shared what was happening in my life, he told me perhaps God was calling me into the ministry. He then gave me great advice and said "don't go and quit your job until you know for sure what God is seeking from you." I've given the same advice to many since that day.

From my meeting with my pastor and following much prayer, I came to the clear conclusion that Jesus was calling me to leave my career as an accountant and give my life to full-time ministry. The question then became: how does a 33-year-old man with a wife and three children, a mortgage, too much credit card debt and too little theological education drop his nets and come follow Jesus?

I began negotiating with Jesus. I figured my situation was different. Besides, at least Peter, James and John didn't have Bank of Israel expecting another house payment on the 14th of every month. So we prayed, I negotiated, and we sought God's guidance on what to do next.

For months we processed the call to surrender our lives to full-time ministry, praying and fasting to determine the will of God. We knew our circumstances were different because of our age and responsibilities, but

God was bigger than every obstacle we could erect. He didn't care about my credentials – or lack thereof – or the fact that I had no formal theological training. God wasn't worried about the age of our children, the mortgage on our home, or the self-inflicted stress we encountered. He simply pursued us around every corner of daily life and every bend in the road. The entire process was delightful and miserable all wrapped into one. Coming to a point of complete and utter surrender is painful. Don't let anyone tell you differently.

We love Jesus and wanted to do His will. Our understanding of God's call upon the rest of our lives was difficult and led to many late night talks and not a few tears. But on that particular Sunday morning it all came together as God had ordained. We both knew it when Andi wrote on the corner of the worship guide, "Let's do it; let's live the adventure!" Surrender had come, and at that moment our bubble popped.

My story is different than yours. The strategy Jesus employs to burst the bubble you've created is unique to you. It's supposed to be! God is so uniquely original in His creativity that He gave you and me different fingerprints, a one-of-a-kind DNA, as well as other characteristics distinctly our own. Why would He use the same strategy in calling you to live outside the bubble you've created as He did with me? He wouldn't. But don't ever think Jesus isn't relentlessly pursuing you to a life above the myriads of "rut-dwellers" who wander about in self-absorbed boredom. He desires to transform your life through a call to live the Gospel as the greatest truth for an overcoming life. He beckons you come follow Him and realize it's all about Jesus! *Simply Jesus!*

# chapter 2
## CHASING STICKS

THE WRITER CHARLES SCHULZ MADE a fortune entertaining the world with his *Peanuts* comic strip. Unless you are from Saturn, you know the exploits of Charlie Brown, Lucy, Sally and Linus. We love them to this day. Most of us get a warm, sentimental feeling when we recall where we were the first time we watched *A Charlie Brown Christmas*. For me, it was delightful and heartbreaking all rolled into one. I loved every second of Charlie seeking to determine what Christmas was all about and when it was over, I was devastated. It ended far too quickly for my liking. My wife cried the first time the show ended when she was a child.

Did I mention Snoopy was unquestionably the coolest dog to ever flash across our televisions? Snoopy was the original hipster before being hipster was hip. He was so cool that he became the icon for many kids when searching for the perfect name for their trusty beagle. Snoopy seemed almost as human as Charlie Brown; he just wore dog fur as opposed to a yellow-and-black polyester blend. He was cool and his cool factor grew exponentially every year.

In one particular comic strip, Snoopy and Linus are out for a stroll. All of a sudden, Linus picks up a stick and lets it fly. As he does, the inner dog of Snoopy wanted to take over and fetch the stick. But Snoopy, being the hipster dog he was, just couldn't lower his standards to those of the non-hipster, regular dogs in the neighborhood. So as he stood unmoved, the caption above him read, "I don't want to be just a nice guy who chases sticks." I like that!

When it comes to the simple Gospel of Jesus Christ, there are numerous, convoluted messages today about what it is and is not. The theological world that I find myself in seems to do everything we can to make the Gospel anything but simple. While intentions are usually good, we provide complex theological constructs regarding Jesus' Gospel and we wonder why so many people check out and don't care to listen to what we have to say. Some people label any good thing the "Gospel truth" seeking to add emphasis to their point of view. Others believe the Gospel has magical powers. Kind of like a sorcerer conjuring up a potion or a lucky rabbit's foot. False promises are made regarding the Gospel that overreach. Many fall short!

If we seek to honor God above all else, the primary goal of every person should be to live daily with a "Simply Jesus" mentality and attitude. The need for confusion regarding the Gospel and what matters most is unwanted. With this in mind, I have one purpose for writing a book entitled "Simply Jesus." In the pages ahead I will provide a simple, thoroughly biblical look into the most important topic on earth – the Gospel of Jesus Christ. I promise not to oversell the Gospel and tell you that if you'll listen carefully, turn around three times, hop back, point upwards and shout hallelujah as loud as you can that you'll win the lottery. Instead, I will share with you something far better than winning the lottery and I will not pull my punches when I do. Stick around and keep reading.

## Don't Waste My Time

Right away some of you may be thinking, "Please, I've been in church all my life. I know what the Gospel is and what it's all about. Don't waste my time, man." I won't waste your time. But if the truth be told when it comes to the simple Gospel, you are probably doing enough of that yourself. I know I have. I have wasted far too much of the precious time God has given me doing many things other than taking seriously the Gospel. (That's called self-confession; it's painful but people say it's good for you.)

I will go out on a limb and say that the vast majority of confessing evangelical believers who would consider themselves good church members waste vast quantities of time when it comes to the Gospel. We are a generation of Jesus followers who have wandered from the path of obedience to stumble down the path of convenience. We are so like Snoopy it's not even funny. We are driven by such a strong desire to appear cool that we've neglected that which we should long to embrace. The majority of confessing Christians in the Church of the Lord Jesus Christ have avoided doing what we've been commanded by our Lord. It's as if we attend church on Sundays and close our ears to the message that matters most. Jesus demands our undivided attention, but we have lost the ability to hear with all the "white noise" and distractions consuming us. We are people chasing sticks!

The Gospel is God's call to the redeemed to stop wasting your time chasing sticks. By its nature it is a call to reject passivity, embrace truth, and turn our fleeting attention to that which is ultimately important. If we understand the Gospel and yet do nothing with that knowledge, how can we claim to be in relationship with Jesus? We are wasting everyday opportunities placed before us by God.

The Gospel is God's clear and undeniable call to "stop chasing sticks" and to honor Him with our entire lives. It is a divine demand requiring all who kneel in allegiance to do something significant all because of the Gospel of Jesus Christ. So whatever you do, don't put this book down. It is going to speak to your heart and life as we travel through "Simply Jesus" together.

## Unashamed

"Paul, a servant of Christ Jesus, called to be an apostle, set apart for the Gospel of God, which he promised beforehand through his prophets in the holy Scriptures, concerning his Son, who was descended from David according to the flesh and was declared to be the Son of God in power according to the Spirit of holiness by his resurrection from the dead, Jesus Christ our Lord, through whom we have received grace and apostleship to bring about the obedience of faith for the sake of his name among all the nations, including you who are called to belong to Jesus Christ. To all those in Rome who are loved by God and called to be saints: Grace to you and peace from God our Father and the Lord Jesus Christ. First, I thank my God through Jesus Christ for all of you, because your faith is proclaimed in all the world. For God is my witness, whom I serve with my spirit in the Gospel of his Son, that without ceasing I mention you always in my prayers, asking that somehow by God's will I may now at last succeed in coming to you. For I long to see you, that I may impart to you some spiritual gift to strengthen you—that is, that we may be mutually encouraged by each other's faith, both yours and mine. I do not want you to be unaware, brothers, that I have often intended to come to you (but thus far have been prevented), in order that I may reap some harvest among you as well as among the rest of the Gentiles. I am under obligation both to Greeks and to barbarians, both to the wise and to the foolish. So I am eager to preach the Gospel to you also who are in Rome. For I am not ashamed of the Gospel, for it is the power of God for salvation to everyone who believes, to the Jew first and also to the Greek. For in it the righteousness of God is revealed from faith for faith, as it is written, 'The righteous shall live by faith.'"

Romans 1:1-17

As Paul writes to Jesus followers in Rome, he is well aware of the difficulties advancing against the Church. Assuming Paul wrote Romans on his third missionary journey in A.D. 57, he would be well aware that the Roman emperor Claudius had expelled Jews from Rome in A.D. 49 because of strife surrounding "Christos." By the times of his writing, Nero would have taken hold of Rome and any student of history knows that this mad emperor had a deep, intrinsic hatred for Jesus followers and the Church. In spite of the deepest of persecutions, Paul declares his unashamed zeal for the Gospel.

God used Paul to define for the Church then and today what the Gospel truly is and what it is not. He removes the mystery surrounding the Gospel and reveals why it is the most important truth the world has ever known. A most profound but simple truth!

## God's Unfailing Promise

From our earliest years, we understand the power of a promise kept and the devastation of a broken one. We begin making pinky promises and crossing our fingers in elementary school. We make promises to friends and to our family. To our parents we may promise something like this: "Mommy and daddy, please can we have the puppy? Please can we have him? We *promise* we're going to brush him every day. We'll walk him. We'll feed him and water him. And mommy, if he poops on the floor, we'll clean it up." All of this is said with the cutest looks of sincerity coming from our little cherubs who have crossed into lawyer mode seeking to sway the hardened jury. The tactic seems to work more often than not.

In this passage, however, God is the one making a promise to us over a matter much weightier than getting a new puppy.

God promised the Gospel in the opening pages of the Old Testament. Paul confirms this in verse 1, "Paul, a servant of Christ Jesus, called to be an apostle, set apart for the Gospel of God, which he promised beforehand through his prophets in the holy Scriptures, concerning his Son..." A little bit later in the same chapter he says, "For God is my witness, whom I serve with my spirit in the Gospel of his Son..." The Gospel of God and the Gospel of his Son are one and the same, an undeniable eternal promise from God.

He said the Gospel was "...promised beforehand through the Scriptures." Go back to the beginning in Genesis 3:15 to the first reference to a coming Redeemer and the first announcement of the Gospel. This verse says, "I will put enmity between you and the woman, and between your offspring and her offspring; he shall bruise your head and you shall bruise His heel." While Paul didn't quote this verse directly, it is highly possible he had it in mind, along with many other Old Testament references that foreshadow the Gospel that was to come thousands of years later. God gives us glimpses of this Gospel throughout the Old Testament so that when Matthew picks up his stylus in the New Testament and we meet the Lord Jesus in vibrant detail, we are not shocked but can clearly see that the Gospel was God's great promise planned from the very beginning.

Some mistakenly think that when Malachi ends the Old Testament, God makes a critical decision for a new beginning at that particular point: "Okay, let me see, what can I do to fix this mess? Oh yeah, I get it. I know what I'll do, I'll send Jesus, My son, and call My plan the 'Gospel.' That's how I'll fix this mess that began so long ago in the Garden." While it is true that the Gospel will fix the "mess" we find ourselves in as a result of Adam & Eve's sin, the Gospel is not the groping response of a desperate God. He's not calling an audible because the demon defense is showing blitz. To believe this reveals a poor understanding of the majesty and sovereignty of God and

His eternal plan. The Gospel is not something God came up with to save the day. God promised the Gospel in eternity past and His vast array of promises can always be trusted.

Years ago someone claimed to have read the Bible and recorded every promise found on its pages. After what must have been an exhausting analysis, he emerged to proclaim there to be 7,000 promises in God's word. While I admire detailed work of this sort, especially when done by someone else, I can't fathom sitting down to list every promise of God from cover to cover. So I took a different research approach, I Googled to see how many promises are found on the pages of Scripture. When I did, Google responded, and everyone knows Google does not lie (insert sarcasm here), that there were 3,573 promises from God. Regardless of whether there is 7,000 or 3,573 or any number in between or even if there were only one promise in the Bible, God's promises never fail! He is trustworthy and faithful. What He says He will do, He does. His promises are always "Yes" because of the Gospel of Jesus Christ. The Bible says in 2 Corinthians 1:20, "For all the promises of God find their Yes in Him."

For God to break even one tiny promise He has made to us, would nullify and void every promise He has ever made. God would never do that. The simple Gospel of Jesus is God's greatest promise and it can never fail.

## God's "Great" Good News

Every person loves good news! When you hear that someone you love but have not seen in a long time is coming home for a visit, that's good news. When you are a student who has studied hard and you pass the exam, that's good news. When you didn't study and you passed, that's really good news!

There's good news, and then there's what I call *great*, good news. The great, good news for grandparents came when your children sat you down and said, "We're going to have a baby, grandma and grandpa." That's great, good news that far surpasses just getting your true/false questions correct in college history. There's good news, and then there's great, good news.

If the New England Journal of Medicine reported tomorrow that a cure for cancer has been found and there would be no more need for chemotherapy or cancer wards in hospitals once a simple vaccination is administered, that's great, good news!

But if I asked you what is the greatest good news this world has ever seen, what would your answer be? If you are sitting in small group bible study, we know the answer would be "Jesus!" because everyone knows that when in doubt just say "Jesus" and you'll probably be correct, at least 50% of the time. But, seriously, what is the greatest good news? Is there good news that surpasses all of the other great, good news combined?

Paul shares the answer to this question in verse 15, "So I am eager to preach the Gospel to you also who are in Rome." He says he is *eager*. That means he is totally pumped up, motivated, excited, prepped and poised to preach the Gospel like Lebron James taking the court for the last game of the NBA championship with the series tied up. Bring it on! What has made Paul so eager?

The word "Gospel" in its simplest form means "good news." Paul is excited and eager to preach to those in Rome because he is bringing them good news. The apostle knew the news he carried with him was far better than the good news of a relative coming home from a long separation, or news of a new baby, or even news that there is a cure for cancer. Imagine that? Now that is *great, good* news!

He was bringing this great, good news to people in desperate need of hope and therefore, he strains with eagerness to preach them the good news! He wanted every person he encountered to at least hear the good news. What they do with what they hear is for another chapter, but Paul was going to do his dead level best to make sure everyone heard the great, good news he came bearing. The simple Gospel of Jesus Christ is God's great "good news" above all else!

When Paul was confronted by Jesus on the road to Damascus, at that moment, his Pharisaical bubble was popped and he ceased chasing sticks. He had no interest in preaching that which was not the Gospel. His eager desire was to preach what he knew would change lives from the inside out for eternity. Paul was a carrier of God's great, good news and God takes the preservation of His Gospel very seriously. In Galatians 1:8, Paul tells us that if anyone declares a different Gospel than the one given by God, let them be eternally cursed. The Gospel is precious and God protects that which is precious.

But why is Paul so eager to preach the good news? It is for one reason – this man had encountered the risen Lord Jesus and had been transformed by the power of the Gospel himself. He knew that it was not for just a select few people, it was for everyone who would open their heart to the call of God unto salvation. Paul was eager because he had internalized the life-changing power of the good news personally and he knew that if those in Rome – and everyone today – heard the good news, their lives could be changed by Jesus also. This is the heart of the matter when it comes to the simple Gospel.

# Debunking Myths

There are many myths regarding the Gospel floating among us today. Let's take a few of them down.

## Myth #1 – *The Gospel is God's advice to eliminate the troubles in my life.*

A self-serving Gospel has been preached for years. The myth that all of our troubles in this life are erased when we answer the Gospel and become Jesus followers has been touted for decades. This reasoning comes from a false understanding that since the Gospel is good news, surely all the troubles one might encounter in life would be negated when the Gospel is received. This is blatantly false.

The Gospel is good news; it is not good advice to remove my daily troubles. God did not provide the Gospel as a source of advice or helpful hints for getting us through tough Mondays, or other tough weekdays. It is also not God's opinion and subject to our receiving or rejecting. Too many see God as nothing more than a heavenly advice columnist somewhat akin to Ann Landers in the sky. Just seek the opinion of God regarding your situation and your troubles will dissolve like pure cane sugar in hot tea.

The error begins when one believes God gives His opinion. Are you kidding me? God has never given His opinion on anything. Nor does God give advice or helpful hints for happy living. God supplies truth! He is the amazing Creator who knows everything and provides us with all truth to live the Christian life. He is not the "Great Spirit" in the sky who offers psychological advice for a nickel like Lucy does from her roadside booth in Charlie Brown.

Matthew 11:28 says, "Come to me, all who are weary and heavy-laden, and I will give you rest." When Jesus uttered these words, he wasn't giving people advice on how to lose weight. He wasn't advising them on a method of fixing their problems and eliminating all their troubles. Problems and suffering are universal to all of us. The primary meaning of this verse is that if we come to Jesus in full surrender, He says "I will set you free so you're not bound by your futile attempts to please God on your own. When you come to me, I will give you rest from the turmoil of religion and your flawed attempts at trying to make God happy through self-effort."

For some readers, now would be an appropriate time to simply accept that as long as your ticker ticks, you will never be 100% trouble-free in this life. Will an understanding of the Gospel help you deal with daily struggles? Absolutely! Is it the ultimate solution for finding freedom from troubles after this life? Of course it is! But the Gospel was never designed to be advice from God to remove all suffering in this life. It has a much greater purpose than that. The Gospel is far more than just God's advice. It is the greatest eternal truth known to mankind!

## Myth #2 – *The Gospel is an appeal to be moral and good in order to please God.*

Tragically, there are those who transpose rules and regulations onto the Gospel so that it is diluted to little more than a call to morality, goodness and self-effort. These people often try to live good lives for His namesake so that God – who is viewed as a smiling and benevolent grandfather rather than one who lives in inapproachable majesty – can sit in heaven and declare how nice and pleasing we are to Him. To fall prey to this myth turns God's great, good news of grace into a lifetime of slavery and work.

Your objection at this point might be, "Are you telling me that I am not supposed to live a moral and good life and can do anything I please?" By no means! In fact, I am telling you that once you comprehend how great the news of the Gospel truly is, you will want to do nothing less than live to please God. There are far too many deceivers who claim the name of Christ but live in such a manner that everyone else looks at them and doubts their claim. There must always be a change in morality and life practices once we understand the Gospel and embrace Jesus Christ, but don't ever mistake the Gospel as God's appeal to be moral and good on your own. We are broken inside and in need of healing. Worse yet, we are spiritually dead and in need of being raised from the dead. The Gospel brings healing and life to every Jesus follower!

## Myth #3 – *The Gospel is a set of rules I must follow to please God.*

At first glance, this might be appealing to some of us who are rule followers at heart. I confess, I'm a rule guy. You may think that had God simply said, "All right, follow these 47 rules I've developed and all will be right in your spiritual world," that you would be one happy camper. That's actually exactly what He did. It's called the Old Testament Law. To follow the rules or Law of God was the desire of every orthodox Jew. They sought to do this for centuries in order to please God. They gave it their fourth-quarter come-from-behind effort, but still came up short in the pleasing God category. It didn't work for Paul and the Jews and attempting to follow rules to please God won't work for you and me either. The Gospel is not a set of rules.

You say, "What about the Ten Commandments? God gave us those as rules to follow and please Him." If you think this, and you believe you have kept the 10 C's, let me be as gentle with you as possible as I describe you in one word… *Failure!* You haven't kept all of God's Top Ten. You may think you have, but you haven't. Didn't we agree earlier that we had all broken at least one promise in our life? Well, then, we've already lied so we have blown it and failed in our attempt to keep the 10 Commandments. That's just one broken rule. What about idolatry, theft, lust, and some of the others. Please don't pretend that you're righteous in God's eyes because of your ability to follow a rule. Paul could not keep God's Law, and he lived among the best "rule followers" to ever walk the earth. Let's not insult God by saying that we can keep His rules. If we could, the Gospel would not be necessary!

*The Gospel is not anything I can do on my own to please God.* When invited to come to "God's party" in Heaven, I don't bring the chips and salsa to earn merit in His sight. I don't make the queso or bring the jalapeno poppers. If I try to do so I may have a burning sensation but it won't be from popping jalapenos! Here's how it works: God invites me to the party, and He says, "Don't bring anything. I've covered it all."

That's what the Gospel is all about. It's not about anything I can do in order to please God, in order to earn favor with Him. If we could do something special on our own to please God, then scrap the Gospel because it's worthless. So many strugglers try to do the best they can in hopes that they have done enough in the end and God will be pleased. They bring their rule oriented life of bondage before God and expect him to be satisfied. If we could be invited to God's party apart from the Gospel, Jesus would not have had to die. We know that's a lie. So the Gospel is not anything I can do in hope that I will please God.

When you study the major world religions other than Christianity – Hinduism, Buddhism, Judaism, and Islam, as well as the cult offshoots of Christianity – you quickly note them to have a one common denominator. Every world religion apart from true Christianity demands its followers carry out a strict regimen of performance oriented tasks to please their god. These are incredibly burdened people because they know they don't measure up. What a miserable way to live when there is good news available.

I heard about this one guy who fits the bill here perfectly. This dude was the most faithful person in the local "church" he attended. He was always there, always going, always participating. He was one of the most noted people in the community because all who met him understood him to be a religious man of great principle. Man, he taught the best Bible studies, and everybody signed up for his small group. If anyone had it going on, he certainly did with his superior level of spirituality.

When he awoke in the morning, his absolute goal was to please God as a determined rule follower. So every day he went rule by rule by rule, checking off the rule list, believing he was earning God's favor and pleasing Him fully. He condemned immorality. He condemned all that he recognized as evil in God's eyes. He even went so far as to condemn the evil he observed in the lives of others. Whatever didn't fit into his rule plan was considered wrong. He was well known outwardly to be very religious, but inwardly, he was a worn down and beaten soul. Let's read how he described himself and the battle deep within…

> "I don't really understand myself, for I want to do what is right, but I don't do it. Instead, I do what I hate. But if I know that what I am doing is wrong, this shows that I agree that the law is good. So I am not the one doing wrong; it is

sin living in me that does it. And I know that nothing good lives in me, that is, in my sinful nature.

I want to do what is right, but I can't. I want to do what is good, but I don't. I don't want to do what is wrong, but I do it anyway. But if I do what I don't want to do, I am not really the one doing wrong; it is sin living in me that does it. I have discovered this principle of life—that when I want to do what is right, I inevitably do what is wrong."

Have you ever been there? That's the New Living Translation of Romans 7 where Paul says, "I love God's law with all my heart. But there is another power within me that is at war with my mind. This power makes me a slave to the sin that is still within me. Oh, what a miserable person I am! Who will free me from this life that is dominated by sin and death? Thank God! The answer is in Jesus Christ our Lord." There's our answer too, *Simply Jesus*.

# Freed by the Gospel

The Gospel is great, good news that I can be set free by Jesus. That's the best news on the face of the earth! It is good news that I do not have to remain a slave to sin, incarcerated by sinful desires that wage war within me. It is great, good news that I do not have to please God by following rules. It is the divine declaration that self-effort is not needed, that I cannot cut it on my own and that I'm not expected to be able to. I will always fall short. I bring zero help to God's party. That's what the Gospel is all about. It's good news that I can be set free.

Luke 4:18, says, "He (God the Father) has sent me (God the Son) to proclaim liberty to the captives, to set the captives free." Jesus came to open the cell doors and set free the miserable souls bound by the broken religious system the Jews had constructed. Paul found this freedom in Christ and he was eager to pass it onto others.

In John 8:32, Jesus says, "Then you will know the truth…" That word *truth*, the truth of God is found only in the Gospel. "You will know the Gospel truth, and the Gospel truth will set you free." That's what we're talking about. You and I can know truth; it is not unavailable to us. Once we know and embrace the truth we hear, we are set free. No wonder when Paul comes to the end of Romans chapter seven, in verse twenty-five he says, "Thanks be to God through Jesus Christ our Lord." He can't control himself. He is overwhelmingly moved by what God has done in releasing him from the bondage of spiritual failure.

A major problem in the Christian church today is that we are no longer moved by the Gospel. Far too many hear the Gospel and respond like this, "What's the big deal? The story ends the same way every time. Jesus always goes to the cross, every time. I've seen Mel Gibson's *The Passion of the Christ* and I don't want to watch it again." We are unmoved people!

It's a tragedy that too many people sit under their pastor's preaching of the Gospel week after week and think, "Okay, I'll just sit here while the pastor rants on about the Gospel one more time. Then we'll go have lunch." If you ever feel that way, go back to the very beginning. The Gospel of Jesus Christ is God's call to stop chasing sticks and honor God with your whole life.

I recently read a quote by Robert Webb concerning 17th century preacher George Whitefield. Webb said, "One of my favorite mental images is of George Whitefield preaching through his tears and saying, 'You are lawbreakers and criminals before a Holy God. And your greatest sin is that you do not even realize that you have offended God with your sin. If you will not weep for your sins, then George Whitefield will weep for you." Have we not arrived at this place in our modern churches today? We are so unmoved by the Gospel that we do not weep for our sins. We do not worry about having offended a Holy God. We play at worship with sin in our hearts and mistakenly think we have God's favor. We are not consumed by passionate worship of this magnificent God who is so much greater than us that if He did not stay His hand we would all perish because of our sin. We are unmoved!

My prayer is that you would stop what you are doing and seek God's face so that once again the Holy Spirit can have His way in your heart and life. Perhaps our prayer should be "Oh God, move us! Move us by Your Spirit to be a people of honor before You. Not an honor based on our own merit. But rather, an honor that comes only through kneeling before You, our God and Maker, for giving us the good news of the Gospel! Thank You God!"

# Stand and Be Counted

Verses 16 and 17 of Romans 1 are two of the greatest verses in all the Word of God. There is so much here to unpack that we will spend several chapters doing so. In verse 16, Paul starts with these few words: "For I am not ashamed of the Gospel...."

To grasp the full meaning of these verses, you must begin with Paul's context for writing. As he presses the quill against the parchment, he prepares a message to the church in Rome during a time of great and terrible persecution. The world of Paul and Matthew, Mark and Timothy was utterly uncivil toward Jesus followers. We think the world today is bad, and in many ways it is, but when it comes to the Gospel, the time of Paul's writing brought much more fear to the Christian than someone living anywhere in the United States today.

What we must not forget is the Romans who controlled the world during Paul's day and in the years following, were accurately accused of feeding Christians to lions. We must not forget the hatred held by Nero for all Christians. From 54 to 68 A.D. Nero ruled Rome and for sport took Christians, coated them in pitch, stuck them on stakes, and struck fire to them so that flaming followers of Jesus would be the ornamental lighting for his outdoor dinner parties. Let's not forget that. We must not dismiss the setting of the early Church when we read the New Testament.

I've met many missionaries throughout the world; some have suffered greatly. They've lost loved ones on the field, and have been arrested and beaten for their beliefs. But none I'm familiar with have been abused and mistreated for the Gospel like Paul. Our daily life is not consumed with fear of being taken outside the city gates like Paul and being killed because we have believed, taught and preached the Gospel of Jesus Christ. There is no place outside of any city in America where Jesus followers are summarily executed. It's not there... yet.

From the start, let's set these verses in their proper context so we can see the type of robust power these verses convey regarding the Gospel. Paul says to the readers in Rome, "For I am not ashamed of the Gospel," regardless of personal threat or hardship. He is using reverse psychology to help them understand that since he is not ashamed, in light of great and imminent danger, Christians everywhere should not be either.

Let's apply Paul's logic to today. People have all sorts of excuses for not sharing the Gospel. As a pastor, I've heard most of them many times. A common excuse goes like this: "I fear for my safety sometimes when I think about sharing the Gospel. They might close the door in my face." Let's hit the delete button on this wrong thinking right now. When that attitude is present, we have succumbed to the hollow threats of our enemy Satan while dismissing the sovereign protection of God. In the "good old USA," people are not going to tar and feather you for believing and sharing the Gospel. Nobody is going to take you to the edge of the city and run you through with a sword because you are a Jesus follower. They're not going to expose you to the elements and feed you to desert coyotes for telling others about Jesus. Perhaps the day will come in America when this will happen – I, for one think we are heading that direction – but as for now, it is still legal on every street in America to speak about your faith.

But if we'll be honest, our problem is not so much fear as it is the curse of *Gospel apathy*. It's not that we're not nice Christian people, or even unconcerned deep down, we're just people chasing sticks. Our churches are full of decent people who confess to love God but are silenced by a foolish fear of rejection. We've taken our eyes off of our God and closed our ears to His commands. Gospel apathy has consumed our lives to the point where the greatest news is no longer news to us anymore. We don't tell others about Jesus because we have taken the good news of the Gospel and converted it to irrelevant news.

Some like to use another excuse and say, "Well now, God has appointed those who are going to be saved and those who are not going to be saved. So whether I tell anybody or not does not make any difference." That's an unbiblical excuse for extreme Gospel apathy. I'm not going to debate the sovereignty of God's call to salvation at this moment; this is not our greatest issue. Our problem is that this greatest of news has been shelved for fear of offending the potential clientele. Even in many of the evangelical churches in America the Gospel is not regularly preached. We are apathetic towards God's good news and we wonder why we do not have spiritual awakening in America. We don't pray about the Gospel's advance. Why should we pray about that which our actions prove to be irrelevant?

## Foolishness

The Gospel is foolish to an intellectual world. You might disagree, but it really is. Let me put it this way: The simple Gospel of Jesus Christ requires no superior level of intellect to be received; it requires faith. On one hand, you can take the most uneducated, unlearned person and they can believe by faith and receive the benefits of the Gospel. On the other, you have extreme brilliance found in the most gifted minds in the world and they too must humble themselves and believe the simple Gospel like everyone else. While vastly different intellectually, both must come to the level ground of the cross to be a Jesus follower. To inherit eternal life, the uneducated man must exercise faith in Christ in the same way that the brilliant man must do so. Both will come to know Jesus by accepting and believing in the Gospel message by faith, or they won't come to know Jesus at all. This is foolishness to many who believe the letters designating their degrees and accomplishments must count for something with God. For those who believe that, are you kidding? You are not a better candidate for the Kingdom of God just because of your academic prowess. In fact, this type of arrogance is proof positive you don't know God and are not a Jesus follower.

As we will see in the coming chapters, to understand the Gospel, you must come face-to-face with the realization that no person is a good candidate for the Kingdom of God without Jesus. Not one of us. If it weren't for Jesus, no one could be saved. Not one of us. The Apostle Paul deals with this in 1 Corinthians 1:18 where he says, "For the word of the cross [meaning the Gospel] is foolishness to those that are perishing, but to us who are being saved it is the power of God [for salvation]." So don't let someone's intellect intimidate you and make you ashamed to share the Gospel. You are only a tool from God's workshop as you open your mouth for Him. He does the work; you're just a tool to assist in completing His master plan for that person's life. Be a handy tool for God!

## A Hated and Eternal Message

The Gospel is a message many people will hate. Jesus explicitly stated people were going to hate His message as well as the messenger. In Luke 21:17 He tells us, "You will be hated by all for my name's sake." He is basically telling

His disciples, "Everywhere you go, people will hate you for preaching My message." People are sometimes ashamed because they don't want to be hated.

Why do some react in hatred towards the Gospel so that we may feel ashamed? It's because, the Gospel raises the stakes to an eternal level. It always moves from the temporal to the eternal, raising the stake to the highest level. When you share the Gospel, you are sharing God's plan for eternal life, not eternal death.

In John 3:15, Jesus says, "...whoever believes in Him may have eternal life." He is referencing Himself. Thus He is emphatically saying, "Whoever believes in *Me* is going to have eternal life." Jesus stakes a claim in this verse, and many others, that He alone is the avenue to Heaven. If He says that through believing in Him any person can have eternal life, would it not conversely read that whoever does not believe in Jesus will not have eternal life? Of course it does and this is a major sticking point for many.

## Decision Demanded

The Gospel always demands a decision. When you understand the power of God at work in salvation, the Holy Spirit of God is engaging the one hearing the Gospel. When someone explains the truth of the Gospel, the person hearing the truth is listening to the outer voice of the one speaking but the inner voice of the Holy Spirit is shouting on a megaphone. The Holy Spirit (neither the preacher, nor anybody else) brings a word at that moment that we hate. It's called *conviction*. The Holy Spirit convicts us to make a decision for Jesus Christ because the Gospel demands a decision. In John 3:18, Jesus says, "Whoever believes in him [meaning Jesus Christ] is not condemned, but whoever does not believe is condemned already, because he has not believed in the name of the only Son of God." God demands a decision from us. Anyone who says a decision is not demanded when the Gospel is heard dismisses the power of the Holy Spirit. He always demands a decision be made by those who hear the simple Gospel.

## Glory to God

The Gospel is God's supreme plan for Him to receive glory. In verse 5, Paul says, "...through whom we have received grace and apostleship to bring about the obedience of faith for the sake of his name among all the nations…" Or, we might read this verse as such, "so that the name of Jesus will be glorified among the nations!"

When we understand the simple Gospel of Jesus Christ, a natural desire to magnify God's glory occurs. The Gospel should be so vivid that we desire to give God glory in every detail of our life. When the living color of the Gospel replaces the dingy, gray life without God, we never get over what He has done for us. We don't move past it because it has now become central to our lives. Every day when I arise, I think of what God has done in granting me the gift of the Gospel and I am moved to give Him maximum glory. All Gospel apathy is erased. After this, we become a herald like the angels who visited the shepherds on the Bethlehem hillside that first Christmas singing, "Glory to God in the highest!"

Because of the Gospel, it should not be the occasional desire of my heart to glorify God; it should be as natural as breathing. I've been changed and saved for all of eternity because of the simple Gospel of Jesus Christ. This great news should make me want to chase after God, pursuing Him with intense determination – kind of like when my baby girl was chased by a vicious dog while riding her bike. Let me explain.

When my family first entered into ministry, we lived in a beautiful parsonage behind the church in a small Southeast Texas town called Spurger. Behind us about 60 or 70 yards another family lived in a small wooden, frame house. Our children sometimes played with theirs since they were all about the same age. Between their house and ours was a large spread of grass that was part of my yard. It was life in the country so the kids played all over the place.

Our neighbors were very poor and had little of material value other than their four walls, a couple of older cars, a hog pen behind their house and plenty of dogs. These were not the kind of dogs who were kept inside. These were outdoor dogs used to hunt hogs in Texas.

The dogs allowed to roam freely were nice… in general. On this one particular occasion, our oldest daughter, Avery, was riding her bicycle over to their house while I was working in the yard, when one particular dog decided to attack my daughter.

As I am working, I hear a blood-curdling scream coming from across the grass near the neighbor's house. I look up, and there is my Avery on her bicycle, pedaling as fast as she can across the grass to get away from the dog. As she pedals, she is screaming for her daddy as loud as she possibly can. I drop everything and start running straight to my baby. The dog is chasing her and I'm running to her rescue.

As the distance between us begins to close rapidly, about 30 feet before I got to Avery, I thought, "We may be in trouble." I took a step to my right, and she turned her bike straight at me to continue riding to her daddy. I took a bigger step to my right and she took a bigger turn to her left. Still tracking! Just before impact and in a moment of resignation, I remember thinking: *You just have to take it. It probably won't hurt for long, but you are definitely going to be run over by your screaming daughter pedaling her bike straight at you like crazy!*

She hit me head on with her bicycle, without applying the brake even a little. I caught her before she flipped off the bike and we both went down in a pile of daddy, daughter and bicycle. It was a catastrophic moment to say the least. Thankfully the dog that had started this debacle must have been amused because he quit barking and just stood there looking at this pile of chaos in front of him.

I share this story to make this point: If we truly understood the simple Gospel of Jesus and the fullness of God's great, good news that Jesus died so our sins could be forgiven, wouldn't we run towards Him with the same passion of my daughter riding towards her earthly daddy? If we could but grasp the benefits of the Gospel and catch even a little glimpse of the beautiful, glorious Kingdom of Heaven and all God has planned for us as Jesus followers, wouldn't we fix our eyes on Jesus and never look away? Wouldn't our life goal become a passionate and intense desire to see God glorified above all? I think if we understood the Gospel as God intends, all Gospel apathy would disappear and His work would be accomplished as we stopped chasing sticks.

# chapter 3
## GOD'S EPIC STORY

HOLLYWOOD UNDERSTANDS THE WORD *EPIC*. These epics are those larger than life productions that often span many years and contain a powerful message. The movie industry knows that when a monumental production occurs so that it can be labeled *epic* there is much to be gained. The deep pockets of film producers are filled to overflowing when movie critics label their project a "major motion picture event of epic proportion."

The actor Mel Gibson knows well the power of an epic film having played the lead in *Braveheart* and *The Patriot* as well as producing *The Passion of the Christ*. All three would fall in the category of epic film dramas. The actor Russell Crowe embraced the same power in the epic film *Gladiator* when he said, "My name is Maximus Decimus Meridius, commander of the Armies of the North, General of the Felix Legions, loyal servant to the true emperor, Marcus Aurelius. Father to a murdered son; husband to a murdered wife; and I will have my vengeance, in this life or the next." If you've seen any of these films, you know just what I'm talking about!

Many years ago, the actor Charlton Heston played the role of Moses in the epic film *The Ten Commandments*. When he stood on the banks of the Red Sea, lifted high the staff of God to part the waters so that the Jewish people could walk across on dry land, it was an epic moment in motion picture history. *The Ten Commandments* was directed by Cecil B. DeMille and was his cinematic masterpiece. It was also the climax of a brilliant career as it was the last movie he would ever direct. This, too, falls in the category of a grand *epic* production.

These are all examples of movies made by men, but what about God's story? Wouldn't it far surpass what any man could conjure up? Does it have epic qualities after all it is the theme of eternity?

Merriam-Webster's Collegiate Dictionary defines the word *epic* as "a long narrative poem in elevated style recounting the deeds of a legendary or historical hero." The Gospel of Jesus Christ surpasses this definition like no other story.

The Gospel is God's grand production of infinitely epic proportion! It is His masterpiece, the culmination of omniscience and omnipotence, in which the love story of all creation is vividly displayed with Jesus being the only true hero. All other nail-biting dramas and heart-piercing stories pale when laid side-by-side with what God has provided through the Gospel. And, no, I'm not overselling the Gospel because there is a characteristic in the Gospel that no other film, book, or poem can claim. What makes this epic Gospel so special? Here is the answer…

*The only power in the universe that raises the dead*
*to life is the Gospel of Jesus Christ.*

In Romans, what we see from the Apostle Paul is his unashamed love and adoration for God that exists solely because he has grasped the eternal importance of the simple Gospel of Jesus Christ.

In Romans 1:16, Paul says, "For I am not ashamed of the Gospel, for it is the power of God for salvation to everyone who believes, to the Jew first and also to the Greek. For in it [meaning, in the Gospel] the righteousness of God is revealed from faith for faith, as it is written, 'The righteous shall live by faith.'" In the pages to follow, I will share with you four truths related to this great, grand, and glorious *epic* Gospel God has given us.

## Creation and Self-Sufficiency in God's Story

When studying the Bible, you always begin with God. Where else would you begin? It's His creation story, is it not? To grasp the story of God, we must rewind the clock and go back to the very beginning, at least to the beginning we have been provided with in God's word. We will start there and work our way forward.

Paul declares himself unashamed of the Gospel because "it is the power of God." He has a deep understanding of the God he worships, recognizing there are no others worthy of his devotion. Paul knows that there is only one God and He alone is self-sufficient. Because we struggle with self-sufficiency, let me tell you about where I make my home, West Texas.

My family moved to this part of the country almost a decade ago, coming from the opposite side of Texas, a place of rolling hills and tall pines. Because of its vast size, we soon learned that all of Texas is not the same. We may all be "Texans" but there are differences throughout the state. While East Texas was heavily wooded and more compact, we found West Texas to be wide open and spread out.

West Texas is a sparse and rugged land of independence and self-sufficiency. For hundreds of years prior to white settlers planting a stake in the ground in the middle 19th century, West Texas was under the control of Native Americans. This region of Texas, parts of Oklahoma and other areas, was known for the wildest, fastest, fiercest, most intolerant and independent Native Americans to ever roam the Staked Plains, the Comanche. They exhibited an unequaled level of self-sufficiency. They thrived off of roaming buffalo herds and deer but could survive off of the carcass of a dead coyote if need arose. They governed themselves with a hierarchical structure as inflexible as it was respected. Fear was a common tactic utilized by the Comanche to maintain their way of life and settlers seeking to move into their land were shown how fierce these warriors could be. If ever a Native American tribe exhibited self-sufficiency, it was the Comanche, the lingering impact of which lives on today in the West Texas culture.

The Native American's were not the only inhabitants to model self-sufficiency in West Texas. We reside in an area known as the Permian Basin. This region has long been one of the largest producers of crude oil in the world. Odessa and Midland exist today because of the black gold that has been flowing from under its ground for many decades. The term "wildcatter" emerged from the Permian Basin as men invested their last dollar drilling wells they were unsure would make. Fortunes were made and lost overnight. If you have ever watched the movie *Giant* starring Rock Hudson and Elizabeth Taylor, you gain a picture of this vast and unruly country known as West Texas.

Because of the struggle to live in a land where oil is plentiful but water is scarce, where rattlesnakes flourish and drought is definite, and where cattle are required to walk great distances between bites of grass, West Texans are nothing if they are not independent, self-sufficient people. The difficulties of life have demanded the residents be people who epitomize the "pull yourself up by your own bootstrap" mentality. We are self-sufficient to the core, and see this as a virtue to be passed onto our children. But is this a good thing?

If you are dealing with oil wells, cattle ranching and rattlesnakes, promoting self-sufficiency in the following generations is good as long as it doesn't replace a healthy dependence upon Almighty God. But when it comes to the grand scheme of life and death, heaven and hell, lost or saved, self-sufficiency ceases being a virtue and becomes a curse regardless of where you reside. There is only One who is truly self-sufficient and it's not us Texans (or any other location for that matter). The only One who is truly self-sufficient is Almighty God.

In verse 16 of Romans chapter one, Paul uses the word "power" to denote the self-sufficiency of God. In the original language, this word is *dunamis* and is where we get our English words *dynamite, dynamo* and *dynamic*. All three of these are apt descriptors of the power that exists within Almighty God!

Certainly, when we think about the Gospel, the power behind the Gospel is Almighty God. People want and seek God's power to work on their behalf. They want God's dynamic power to work in their life. Some attend crusade after crusade and a multitude of healing services to find God's power for living. I believe in crusades and prayer and God's ability to heal, but if you are a Jesus follower, God's dynamic power *has* worked in your life, and it *is* working in your life. He is at work in our lives all the time.

Tragically, many wrongly assume that by embracing the Gospel we are giving to God something He is lacking. Some preachers regularly communicate that the Gospel's intent is so God can receive the glory He is missing, the glory He needs. While I strongly believe in bringing glory to God, I also know God doesn't need me to achieve glory for Himself. Maybe you've heard someone say, "God sent His one and only Son so you could be saved because God *needs* your worship in heaven." That is fundamentally, theologically and absolutely wrong. Here is the truth...

### God needs nothing from you and me!

Because God is amazingly self-sufficient, He needs nothing! Since He is the awesome, glorious, amazing, wonderful, self-sustaining, self-sufficient

God described in the Bible, then what would He need from you and me? He doesn't *need* our worship. He doesn't *need* our praise. He doesn't *need* our prayers. He doesn't *need* our talents. He doesn't *need* our speaking abilities. He *needs* nothing!

We mistakenly think that our relationship with God is somewhat the relationship we have with our pets. We have two German Schnauzers who lay about our house all day doing nothing. They may get up and occasionally stretch, drink a little water or eat a bite of food. But because they are alone all day, they mostly sleep! When I arrive home in the evenings they rush to the door to greet me with barks and stubby tails wagging. They jump on me and want attention. If I will reach down and give them a pat on the head, that's all they need. They are set for the evening and life is good because I've given them what they needed.

Too many in church mistakenly think God needs our worship like my dogs need a pat on the head at night. They believe that if we'll just give God the occasional pat on the head and scratch Him behind the ears, He will be satisfied and happy. That's wrong thinking and horrible theology!

When God created Adam, the purpose of the creation was not to fill a gap missing in God's life. The Holy Trinity – God the Father, Son and Holy Spirit – were not huddled before creation trying to find the missing link as to what they needed to make them happy. God was absolutely content in who He was then and who He is today. He is not missing anything, and that includes our worship.

So when Paul writes that he is not ashamed of the Gospel, he is writing with full knowledge that he doesn't fill a gaping hole in God's psyche. He doesn't complete God or make Him better. In every way God has shown Paul abounding grace through the Gospel message and salvation, but neither Paul nor you or I plug our finger into the leaking levy of God's emotions. God has no flaw or need. He is totally self-sufficient.

It is a humbling moment when a person comes to the recognition that God does not need them. God didn't need Paul. He doesn't need me as a pastor. He doesn't need you who read this book. Because He is self-sufficient, God needs nothing!

The book of Romans is considered the greatest theological book in the New Testament. When you begin to study the New Testament and you come to Romans, you encounter theological truth spread before you like a savory banquet table loaded with exquisite cheeses, lavish meats and every French pastry known to man. When you roll through the first eight chapters of Romans, God supplies everything we need to know for sound theology and our understanding of the Gospel. He explains that we're all sinners and in need of His grace in order to be cleansed and declared righteous.

God supplies all of that in Romans, chapters one through eight. By the time Paul has arrived at Romans, chapter nine and he begins to unfold the mystery of the Gospel in even greater detail, he seems overwhelmed with both God's goodness and His grace. So much so that when he concludes chapter 11, he bursts forth with unhindered praise to the self-sufficiency of Almighty God. Look at the words the Holy Spirit inspires Paul to write in conclusion of Romans 11: "Oh, the depth of the riches and wisdom and knowledge of God! How unsearchable are His judgments and how inscrutable His ways! 'For who has known the mind of the Lord, or who has been His counselor?' 'Or who has given a gift to Him that He might be repaid?' For from Him and through Him and to Him are all things. To Him be glory forever. Amen."

So, let's get this truth indelibly planted in our minds right now. God gives us the Gospel as an act of His grace so we might be saved, not because He needs something from you and me. God needs nothing. God is our totally self-sufficient Creator. He is self-sustaining. And here's the unmatched blessing of what this self-sufficient God has done. When I give my heart to Jesus Christ by answering the call of the Gospel by faith, while He needs nothing from me, He gives me everything!

God gives me eternal life, God washes me clean from my sin, and gives me a place in heaven where I will worship him for eternity, not because He needs it, but because I have the most delightful privilege of getting to do it. Do you see what I'm saying? We must begin with God in this great, grand, epic drama called the Gospel if we are going to understand His story.

## The Nightmare on Eden Street

In 1984 a popular horror movie hit the box office called *A Nightmare on Elm Street*. The movie tells the story of teenagers trapped between their dreams and reality as they are systematically targeted by a horrible villain named Freddy Krueger. With long blades coming from his fingers, Krueger slashes, cuts and destroys in a nightmare of perverted fantasy.

Long before this movie hit the big screen, there was a nightmare that happened in the Garden of Eden, *The Nightmare on Eden Street*. To understand why Paul is not ashamed of the Gospel, you must go to the beginning of God's epic creation story. I have labeled it *The Nightmare on Eden Street* because there the original villain, far more evil than Freddy Krueger, attacked and sought to destroy God's children. There Satan tempted them to sin, and they gave into temptation. In this most horrific nightmare, evil entered and began to flourish on earth.

Paul says, "For I am not ashamed of the Gospel, for it is the power of God for salvation." The Gospel delivers us from the horrible nightmare of that fateful day when Satan tempted Eve and Adam followed her into temptation. On that day, sin entered the world and every one of us since then has been born with a sin nature inherited from our first parents. We are born with it inside of us. We have the capacity to do evil even more than we have the capacity to do good. We all have it inside of us; none are exempt.

That's why Paul unequivocally states in Romans 3:23 that "...all have sinned and fall short of the glory of God." All of us! That's also why, as we study the Gospel, we come to the realization that Romans 6:23 strikes the center mass of the bullseye as it describes the fate of every person because of sin - "the wages of sin is death." We will all die because of sin. We'll die a physical death and a spiritual death as a result of sin if something or someone doesn't come forth to set us free.

This is the curse of *The Nightmare on Eden Street*. There is nothing on our own we can do about it, nothing! Can you imagine? We are in a flawed situation that we are powerless to correct. Some situations we experience in life we cannot fix ourselves.

When our son, Jordon, was five years old, he was a lean, fleet-footed little fellow. He played hard every day and when his head hit the pillow he was out like a light. One day Andi noticed that Jordon was a little thicker around the middle. She asked me if I'd observed Jordon's seemingly overnight weight gain. Being the oblivious dad I am, I missed the medical alarm bells and told her that he was just filling out and buffing up with some additional muscle. She was not to be deterred. Andi knew something was wrong.

The next day she called our pediatrician and we found ourselves driving the 100 plus miles to see Dr. Don. When we arrived that Friday morning, he did an exam along with a urinalysis. In just a short time he told us we needed to see a renal specialist that day. It was Friday and doctors had closed up shop for the week, but after pulling some strings and throwing his weight around, Dr. Don had us an appointment for early afternoon. In the meantime he told us to go grab a bite of lunch and he'd be in touch.

Since we no longer lived in Houston and didn't have tasty Tex-Mex close by, we headed to a local Mexican joint to fill up on chips, salsa and enchiladas. When we sat down, Jordon began emptying the salt shaker directly onto his chips. He'd never done this before and, of course, we made him stop. He drank tons of water, ate a little of his meal and we headed out the door to our next appointment. As we got back to our van, Jordon vomited everything everywhere. It was at that moment that even this usually obtuse daddy realized everything was not as it should be.

Upon arrival at the specialist's office, they took Jordon's blood pressure and found it to be 195/120. They immediately gave him something to begin bringing it down. It was then the renal specialist told us Jordon had acute nephritis and that we'd be staying at Texas Children's hospital that night. Fact is we stayed the next 4 nights as they monitored his kidneys and sought to keep him from having permanent damage to his renal system.

As a mom and dad, we found ourselves in a situation we could not fix on our own. We were helpless to do anything physically for our son to make him better. We didn't have the medical training or the access to the necessary drugs to fix Jordon's problems. While I'm a doctor (my kids have laughingly told me I'm not the kind that really helps people), my theological education couldn't help us at all. We were at the mercy of someone else stepping into our lives to fix what was impossible for us to fix on our own.

Every person since Adam and Eve has been diagnosed with spiritual failure by God and are in a place where they can do nothing to fix their problem themselves. *The Nightmare on Eden Street* has slashed their spiritual life to shreds and apart from the Gospel there can be no healing because we've all sinned, and the wages of sin is death. Romans 3:23 shows us we are living a horrible nightmare apart from God!

Have you ever been caught up in a dream that just won't stop but goes on and on? I don't have too many bad dreams, but not long back I did. I don't remember the details, but I remember waking up in the wee hours of the morning, getting out of bed and thinking, "Wow! I'm glad that's over with." You've done that too, right?

Do you know what happened? When I went back to sleep, I went right back into my bad dream, picking up right where I'd left off. Talk about miserable! Have you ever done that? It's a horrible feeling. You want to wake up from this dream that's bad, but you can't. That's how it is with *The Nightmare on Eden Street*, we want to wake up from the dream, but apart from God we can't wake up. We cannot beat our sin nature on our own. We cannot make ourselves good enough and pleasing to God on our own. We are trapped in a nightmare that will not stop.

It's like what the prophet Jeremiah said in chapter 13, verse 23. He says, "Can the Ethiopian change his skin or the leopard his spots?" The answer is an emphatic, "No, absolutely not!" It can't happen. We cannot atone for our sin any more than the Ethiopian can change his skin or the leopard his spots. We are sinners in the middle of a nightmare that will not end apart from one thing… the simple Gospel of Jesus Christ!

The Story of God tells us that He sent his only Son so sinners could be saved and delivered from this horrible nightmare. It tells us God allowed his Son to die in our place, suffering unspeakable wrath so we might be awakened and set free. Only because of the power of the Gospel can the chains be removed and freedom found from this horror show called *The Nightmare on Eden Street*.

But it gets even better! Once you wake up, because you've received Jesus Christ by faith, because you've been delivered from that horrible nightmare, you never re-enter the bad dream again, ever. It's all about the power of Almighty God working on our behalf so that we may be saved. No wonder Paul says, "I'm not ashamed of the Gospel," because he comprehends its glorious power. He understands the Gospel from three different angles.

## Delivery from Sin's Guilt

Before I trust Jesus Christ for eternal life, God looks at me and sees a guilty sinner, unable in any way to find release and freedom from this guilt. If I were to appear before Him at that moment He would look upon me and say, "You're a guilty sinner. You are guilty in my sight. And because you're guilty, you deserve death and will receive death."

The Gospel is powerful because it delivers me completely from the guilt of sin. Once I accept Jesus Christ as my Lord and Savior, having believed in the Gospel message by faith, regardless of the curse of sin that I had been carrying, God stamps me "not guilty" from that point on. I am delivered from the guilt of sin from that point forward in the eyes of God.

## Delivery from Sin's Power

Upon believing the good news, we do not have to be in bondage to sin anymore. While Satan will always pull our strings, he no longer has the power to win because we stand in the victory won by Jesus. Satan has been defeated, and we can now live in the freedom that comes through Jesus Christ and in Him alone. John, chapter 8, verse 36, says, "When the Son sets you free, you're free indeed." So I am released, and I am free. I find that freedom because I'm no longer bound by sin dominating my life.

Since I've been talking about horror movies, think of it like this. Have you ever watched a suspenseful, nail-biting horror movie that almost suffocates you with fear and then breathed a huge sigh of relief when the evil villain appears to be killed? You've been there, right? But just when you think you can now begin breathing normal again, this hideous creature we thought was dead decides to come back for another round. Why we do not learn from past experience and say, "He's coming back, he's coming back!" I'll never know because he always does.

That's the way it is spiritually. Before you come to know Jesus Christ, sin has you bound and incarcerated. Because you don't have the power of the Gospel working on your behalf, you can't be set free on your own. But once you believe by faith and are forgiven and released, even though sin no longer binds you, Satan still comes back around to seek to defeat you every chance he gets. The difference now, however, is that the power that saved you is also what sustains and protects you so that you may now walk in daily victory.

## Delivery from Sin's Pollution

Do you wonder why we have things like the Zimmerman-Trayvon Martin ordeal in America? Has it registered with you why the 2009 massacre at Fort Hood took place, or any school shooting for that matter? Does it not appear that multitudes will go to no end every day to have their sin sated with drugs, alcohol, pornography and other deviant forms of behavior? All of these that

I have described are ultimately the result of sin and the pollution it brings to our life and society. Do you wonder why racism exists, prostitution, or sexual trafficking? Again, it's all because of sin, the ever-increasing pollution of sin that began way back in the Garden of Eden so long ago.

The same goes for bigotry and hypocrisy in America. It is because of sin. Do you wonder why marriages implode around us all the time? Do you wonder why children are abused and neglected? It's because of the pollution of sin.

My son and I love to camp. We sit by the fire and then go into our tent where we have it gently lit with coal oil lamps. When you light the lamp, if the wick is turned up too high the flame will be too large and produce a thick black smoke called soot. The soot from the flame will then coat the inside of the glass globe so that the light inside is hardly visible. That's a picture of the pollution of sin in our land. It coats everything like soot covering the inside of the globe.

When you consider the impact of sin that dates back to *The Nightmare on Eden Street*, no wonder Paul is not ashamed of the Gospel. Nothing can eclipse what he has been delivered from through the Gospel and therefore he is so unashamed that he will die before he is silenced. Why is this? Because Paul realizes what he has been delivered from.

## Rescue Mission

*The Nightmare on Eden Street* goes on and on and on. It is so terrifying that apart from the simple Gospel of Jesus Christ all will burn in hell for eternity. Is it any wonder why Paul is so consumed with the Gospel? He is unashamed because he is keenly aware that Jesus rescued him from a sure eternity in unquenchable fire. He says in verse 16, "For I am not ashamed of the Gospel, for it is the power of God for salvation."

Most can grasp that the word *salvation* means to be saved from something by someone. When a life-threatening event occurs and someone steps forward to rescue us from imminent danger, we overflow with thankfulness and call the person our hero. When it comes to eternal salvation, Jesus Christ is the Hero of the story! He stepped out of His palace in Heaven, across the stars of eternity and down into a manger in Bethlehem born to a virgin named Mary. He came for one reason only, to rescue His creation from the horrors of hell. He brings salvation to those who call upon Him by faith because no person is capable of saving himself. Let me explain our dilemma.

When I was a boy growing up in East Texas, several of our extended family lived in the same small town. We are a close family and have always volunteered to help one another when the need arises and there was work to be done. One of the chores I enjoyed in the winter was going with my granddad to feed my uncle's cows. The green grass in the pastures was long gone and if you neglected to hay your cattle, they would not get enough to eat. So every day or so we would head to the barn where we'd load bales of hay into the back of my grandpa's truck and drive into the pasture to put the hay on the ground for the cattle who always came running with hungry bellies.

After you've done this for a while, you become familiar with the cows. You know what to look for to ensure all of the cattle are present and accounted. When one is missing, you know something could be wrong. One day my grandpa noticed a cow missing from the herd and decided we needed to look around for her before we left.

As we left the cows happily eating their hay, we drove into the pasture searching for the cow we knew was missing. When we drove to the backside of the pasture, we arrived at a large hole in the ground, a pit about 8 feet deep. When we walked up to the side of the pit, we looked down, and looking up from the bottom were two huge cow eyes and two big ears sticking up as if to say, "Can you believe the mess I've gotten myself into. It's about time you came to get me out!"

There was no way on God's green earth that cow was coming out of that pit by herself. She had tried to jump out, but couldn't do it. She had tried to climb out, but hooves don't grab very well when climbing up a dirt wall. She had tried everything possible and failed every time. There was no way she was getting out of the pit on her own. If someone didn't rescue her, she'd die right there in a pile of cowhide, bones, hooves and horns. Do you see the dilemma?

We didn't have cell phones back then so we went to the closest pay phone and called my Uncle Toby, informing him that his cow was stuck in a huge hole in the ground. He said, "I'll be there in a few minutes," which meant he would show up quite a while later. We waited in the truck until he finally showed up to save the cow.

When he arrived, we stood looking down at the cow as she continued looking up in desperation. We brainstormed ideas on how to get her out, but none seemed plausible except one. All we had were the pickup trucks and some rope. How are you going to get this cow out of the pit with just a pickup and a rope? You may not like the solution we came up with, but he threw a rope around the neck of that cow, tied it to the truck, cranked it and punched it. Quite amazingly, that old cow learned to jump like Michael Jordan about the same time she hit the end of the rope and in seconds was out of the pit.

After she was dragged out of the pit, she obviously needed a moment to get her bearings. She lay there with her tongue hanging out while we unhooked the rope. Then, almost as if on cue, she got up, shook her head and trotted off towards the other cows to eat some hay. She was saved!

There are probably some of you reading this aghast at the brutal tactic we used to save that cow. You're thinking, "I can't believe you'd be so cruel as to drag that cow out of the pit by the neck." The very fact that we'd risk breaking her neck or choking her to death along the way may be appalling to you on many different levels. How anyone could be so cruel to that poor cow is unimaginable. Before you pick up the phone to call P.E.T.A., check this out.

Has it occurred to you that she would've died had we left her in the pit? She would have died a lingering and agonizing death due to starvation in just days had we driven home and decided we didn't want to risk hurting her neck. Would that have been better? Which is crueler, leaving her in the pit to die or dragging her out so she can grab a few bites of dinner before the other cows eat all the hay?

Here's the problem today regarding salvation and the preaching of the Gospel. Far too many preachers proclaim a "leave them in the pit" form of the Gospel. After all, we wouldn't want to preach that there is a literal hell because that would be unpopular and even seen as cruel. We would not want to address the biblical fact that there could truly be a place where real people we know and love could actually spend an eternity burning in the fires of hell. No, we wouldn't want to mention that, so instead we just "leave her in the pit" and go about our business treating God's great story known as the Gospel as if it's some sordid fairytale we can take or leave.

I hope that since you have read this far, you are beginning to know my heart. You know that I am not afraid to address this very touchy subject. In fact, I hold a firm belief that every preacher given the task of proclaiming God's word who refuses to preach on hell is an offense to God and a snare to the eternity of those who listen. Every week when the preacher steps to the pulpit there are sinners stuck in the pit just like that old cow. They are dying and unable to save themselves from the future torment the Bible promises for the lost. They cannot climb or jump out. To only preach on how to be happy in life, how to have a happy marriage, or how to have sex God's way, and to never address that which is of eternal importance, is an injustice before God!

The Gospel was sent by God to rescue people out of a pit of death and into the glorious light of an eternity in Heaven. Isn't that good news to you?

Of course, here is where that same group of naysayers will shout, "My God is a loving God. He wouldn't allow any person to suffer an eternity in hell."

God is an incredible God of love. God loves you so much that he sacrificed his Son for you. He sent his Son to die as the supreme act of love, never to be equaled again. He is most assuredly a God of love, but He is equally a God of incredible severity and wrath. If you deny his Son and do not receive him by faith, you will justifiably spend an eternity separated from God in hell.

## Hell's Reality

Jesus unashamedly taught on hell! He knew He was the only solution for delivering us from hell. He taught on hell regularly in His Word. For example, in Matthew, chapter 18, verses 8 and 9, Jesus says, "And if your hand or your foot causes you to sin, cut it off and throw it away. It is better for you to enter life crippled or lame than with two hands or two feet to be thrown into the eternal fire."

Pause for a moment. Do you realize what he's saying? It would be better to have a hook on the end of your arm than to have two functioning hands and live willfully in sin and go to hell. It would be better if you never had feet that you could get up and walk about than to have two feet and live in disobedient rejection of Jesus and go to hell. It would be better if you never had either of these things than to be thrown into the eternal fire.

In verse 9, he says, "And if your eye causes you to sin, tear it out and throw it away." Is this not graphic what Jesus is teaching? Imagine this visually in your mind and the serious nature of his message begins to take shape. Jesus pulls no punches. He says, "It is better for you to enter life with one eye than with two eyes to be thrown into the hell of fire."

I taught this to a group of high school students recently and the looks on their faces were priceless. I could see them asking, "Pastor, does that mean I should go pluck my eye out so I don't go to hell?" No, don't go pluck your eyes out. There's a better solution. The solution is Jesus Christ and His Gospel! We don't cut our hands or feet off and we don't pluck out our eyes. Instead, we trust in Jesus Christ for eternal life.

Jesus speaks of the "hell of fire" at the end of verse 9 using the word *gehenna,* a word you may be familiar with. *Gehenna* was a literal place on the south side of Jerusalem where the masses would go to dump all of the trash from the city. All the waste, all the garbage, the filth and the nastiness that people and animals created was thrown in this place so that it could be incinerated. When the pile would get big enough, they would set it on fire.

Eventually, the fire of *Gehenna* burned continually, never going out; it just smoldered. It was a stinking, rotten, putrid, nasty place. Nobody wanted to go there. If you have ever been to a large city dump, it would be somewhat equivalent to that, only worse. Jesus is using that to illustrate what hell is going to be like, this horrible, nasty, putrid place of burning, where the fire never goes out. It is a very real and literal place.

I'll take you one step further. In Luke, chapter 12, Jesus talks about who we should fear. Remember Paul had said, "I'm not ashamed of the Gospel." Why do we get ashamed? We're afraid to share the Gospel for fear of someone being offended. Our attitude is more often this than anything else, "I wouldn't want to offend anybody, so I don't want to tell anybody about the Gospel." In verse 5 Jesus says, "I tell you, my friends, do not fear those who kill the body, and after that have nothing more that they can do. But I will warn you whom to fear: fear Him who, after He has killed, has authority to cast into hell. Yes, I tell you, fear Him!"

Who is Jesus talking about? None other than Almighty God; only God has the full and complete authority to cast someone into hell. Jesus says, "You fear Him, the one who has the authority to cast you into hell" but you say, "I don't want to fear God."

Tune in carefully to what you read next… I have been very clear that I believe fully in a loving God because the Bible teaches that God is fully and completely loving. But you need to understand that just because you and I believe in a loving God, this does not dismiss the fact that God is also one of severity for those who reject the Gospel message! Any person who hears the good news of Jesus and refuses to become a Jesus follower has thrown the love of this great and glorious God into the sewer and deserves hell.

Since the Bible teaches that God is both love and severity, why in the world do we parents just talk about a loving God to our children but never teach them that there are consequences to our disobedience and rejection of God. Do you not realize what Jesus is saying in these verses 4 and 5? He says, "You're afraid of man when you should have this fear that God could cast you into hell if you don't receive the Gospel."

You mean we are afraid to share this great, good news called the Gospel because we're afraid a mere man or woman may say, "Would you just keep your religious opinions to yourself?" Yet we don't have a healthy fear of God. That's ludicrous!

## New Life in Jesus Christ

This is the culmination of God's great, grand and glorious epic known as the Gospel. This is His theme in eternity, His drama that He planned since before the creation of this world and for centuries now has brought salvation and new life in Jesus. Again, no wonder Paul will say, "For I am not ashamed of the Gospel, for it is the power of God for salvation."

It's all about salvation; being saved. It is being dragged out of the pit you are confined to the freedom of having your sins forgiven. The Gospel is about salvation. It's about deliverance from hell. It is God's act of saving those bound for an eternal hell by taking that which is totally dead spiritually and breathing new life into them.

Anytime someone calls on Jesus by faith, they invoke His power to work on their behalf for the purpose of receiving His salvation in their life. So as I draw this chapter to a close, let me define biblical salvation for you…

Biblical salvation is the redemption of sinners who are spiritually dead from the consequences of *The Nightmare on Eden Street* by granting them new life through Jesus Christ alone by grace through faith.

It is embracing God's epic story of the Gospel and believing by faith what the Bible says regarding sin, self, repentance and the saving work of Jesus on the cross.

Martyn Lloyd-Jones knocks it out of the park with the following picture of God's grand epic known as the Gospel: "Here is the theme of eternity. We are all wretched, we are all foul. What if the world knew your imaginations and your thought; what if your neighbors knew the things that you fondle in your heart? We are all vile, lost sinners, but we have got to stand before a holy God who is a 'consuming fire.' How can we do it? What about the stains on your soul, what about the chastity and the purity you have lost, what about the foulness that has entered into you … What will you do about it? How will you remove it and erase it? And you cannot! But here is a new covenant, mediated by the Son of God. He has shed His precious blood on the Cross of Calvary's hill." [2]

> His blood can make the foulest clean,
> His blood availed for me.
> Charles Wesley

Only by the blood of Jesus are our sins forgiven. Only are the sins forgiven of those who recognize a need for salvation and forgiveness. Only by confessing Jesus by faith is one brought from death to life, from darkness into eternal light.

I said in the opening pages of this chapter that this epic Gospel is the most powerful force on earth. What makes this epic Gospel so special? Here is the answer again…

> *The only power in the universe that raises the dead*
> *to life is the Gospel of Jesus Christ.*

Because of the sacrifice of the Son of God, His burial and ultimate resurrection, we too can be raised to walk as new creations of God. It doesn't matter if we are 10, 20, 30, or 100, salvation is available when one hears the inner call of the Holy Spirit and responds by faith.

Paul grasped this incredible, life giving power in First Corinthians 1:17 when he says, "For Christ did not send me to baptize but to preach the

---

2    Martyn Lloyd-Jones, *The Kingdom of God* (Wheaton, IL: Crossway Books, 1992 by Bethan Lloyd-Jones), 217.

Gospel, and not with words of eloquent wisdom lest the cross of Christ be emptied of its power." In other words, it's not about words of eloquent wisdom that draws a person to Christ. Just embrace the simple Gospel message that Jesus Christ came into this earth, lived a sinless life, died on the cross, rose again on the third day, and is seated at the right hand of God the Father today. That's the message of eternal power that brings the dead to life!

Listen to the evidence of this power as these verses go on, "…our Gospel came to you not only in word, but also in power and in the Holy Spirit and with full conviction." Therein is the answer to why when you read words such as these, if you don't know Jesus Christ and yet in your heart you feel conviction, the conviction does not come from the preacher. The conviction comes through the Holy Spirit speaking to your heart and saying, "Unless you repent of your sins and turn away from the life you're living and turn to Jesus Christ, you will die."

This great, grand, glorious, epic drama of God has been carried out and is continuing to be carried out with God as the writer and director, with the evil villain being Satan, and the Hero being the Lord Jesus. Only the Hero can rescue anyone from the pit of death and despair. Salvation is available until the divine Director comes to the end of His story and says, "That's a wrap." At that moment, the only thing that will matter for every person will be your answer to this question: *What did you do with Jesus Christ when you heard the Gospel?*

Did you accept Him or did you not? Did you believe upon the name of Jesus for salvation or did you figure you can earn a place in Heaven by who you are or what you can do for God? We'll talk about that in the next chapter as we look at God's salvation and our empty hands.

# chapter 4
## EMPTY HANDS

THE SIMPLE GOSPEL OF JESUS Christ is God's oldest story. It
was not developed 2,000 years ago by God to fix a crack in His eternal
plan for Creation. God never says "oops" or needs to fix anything. He did not
launch the Gospel as His last regal attempt to stop the advancing armies of
evil so evident when Jesus walked the earth, resolutely heading towards the
cross. It was always the plan of God to send His Son so that God the Father
would receive maximum glory when creation would look to God the Son for
salvation. As we've already seen, the oldest story is the Gospel story, and as
you might imagine, it has also been the most contested story.

In the mid-to-late 1700's, a young man placed his faith in Jesus Christ
and was soon drawn to the teachings of John and Charles Wesley. Being
enthralled with the Wesley brothers' new "Methodist" movement, he began
to study and grow as a disciple under their tutelage. As time passed, this
new Jesus follower increased in his devotion and found that he differed
theologically with the very ones he once saw as heroes of the faith, the
Wesley's. The theological bone of contention was the Gospel of Jesus Christ.

In the red corner, the Wesley's came out swinging a Gospel of free will.
They held that God had granted free will to every man so that any person
could come to Jesus for salvation at whatever time they deemed appropriate.
In the blue corner, Augustus Montague Toplady brought forth vehement
denials of this strong belief in the free-will of man. He countered with God
being totally sovereign over salvation, so much so that apart from a divine
call there could be no saving grace found by the sinner.

In 1776, while our founding fathers were writing the Declaration of
Independence, Toplady was writing a hymn to counter the teachings of

the Methodists. He wrote the words to what some believe to be one of the greatest hymns found in the Christian church as a lyrical argument against John and Charles Wesley. The hymn is *Rock of Ages*. When reading the words, the second stanza vividly puts forth Toplady's belief regarding salvation and the Gospel. It reads as such:

*Nothing in my hand I bring; simply to Thy cross I cling.*

These words support the Gospel of empty hands.

# Main Event

The Gospel is the central focus of Christianity. If not for the Gospel we would not have a Christian faith, a bible, the Christian Church, or the prospects of divine deliverance from hell. The Gospel is the foremost means through which God receives glory today on planet earth. It is Satan's nemesis and the Church's business. The Apostle Paul was so moved by the main event known as the Gospel that he professed to be totally unashamed of this incredible good news he had received from God. In the first chapter of Romans, verse 17, Paul writes, *"For in it [the Gospel] the righteousness of God is revealed from faith for faith, as it is written, 'the righteous shall live by faith.'"* This righteousness Paul presents is the basis for our understanding of the Gospel of empty hands. It is the main event that demands attention today just as it did 2,000 years ago when Jesus walked this earth in bodily form.

## "Good People" and God's Righteousness

I have met many people that I would call "good people" according to the world's standard of goodness. Many of these I would label kind, generous, gracious, friendly, compassionate, philanthropic, and the list goes on. They are usually not contentious or mean-spirited, but seek to help their friends and be a blessing to others in many ways. These are what we call in West Texas, "just good ol' folks!" And according to worldly standards, these folks *are* good. They may even be called godly or saintly because of the good things they do and the kindness they show to others.

These good people may be ones who knock on your door in the afternoon wearing white shirts and black pants and carrying *The Book of Mormon* under their arm. They could just as well be some so impassioned about their religion that they come bearing copies of *Watchtower Expositor* magazine. Both of these groups would be considered good in the eyes of society, and yet, is this how God defines goodness and are these "good people" in tune with the righteousness of God? Let's find out what passes as "good" in the eyes of God.

God's righteousness and man's righteousness are two totally different kinds of righteousness. The goodness I've described above is worldly goodness that, apart from Jesus Christ, is not considered "good" at all in the eyes of One who is totally holy and righteous. The righteousness of human behavior apart from Jesus is anything but "righteous" in God's eyes. Regarding humanity, Romans 3:10 says, "None is righteous, no, not one." Even Jesus declared in Mark 10:18 that "no one is good except God alone."

Let me illustrate what I mean. When I was a teenager, my mother would sometimes have me vacuum her car. I hated this job. It was not that I minded work; it was just that I minded *this* work. I would usually spend most of my time choking the vacuum cleaner as I attached it to my arm or hand. You have to be really careful here because if you attach it to your neck for too long you will have people thinking badly of you. (It's okay to smile now!)

Here's my vacuuming dilemma, I was never very good at determining just how good Mom's car had to be vacuumed in order to please her. Ten out of ten times I would do my job and call Mom for her inspection. Ten out of ten times she would tell me that wasn't "good" enough and I would go back to vacuuming some more. This was so frustrating to me. I had my definition of goodness and Mother had hers. Why could she not just adjust her standards a little? She never did! What I came to learn was that Mom's standard of cleanliness was not my standard of cleanliness. Make sense?

## One-to-a-Million

On a level far more important than vacuuming a car, many have been fooled into thinking that the world's righteousness and God's righteousness are really the same thing. We may find ourselves at different points on the righteousness scale, but at least we were on the same scale. When many think of God they think of Him being *really* righteous, and in our desire to be humble, we know that we are not nearly as righteous as God. Oh, we do a few good things here and there, so at least we are on the righteousness scale.

Let's imagine for a moment that you could place God's righteousness on a scale of one-to-a-million. We would probably all agree that God is firmly standing on the one million mark. You may struggle with this if you are one who wrongly thinks that Jesus sinned while on this earth or if you are mad at God for not answering those five prayers you've had on your prayer list for a while. In truth, however, the Bible teaches that God is so righteous no other person is even close on the righteousness scale. For this rather poor example, He is the only one standing on the million mark and there are no others that even come close.

On the other end of the one-to-a-million Righteousness Scale, since God is at a million for this example because He's perfectly righteous, we would then all agree that Satan is a zero. Since he's a liar, thief, and murderer, he's a zero in more ways than we can count.

The question now begs to be answered: Where do you find yourself fitting on the one-to-a-million Righteousness Scale? If God stands on one million and the devil is on zero, where are you? Think really hard about all the good things you've done, you don't want to miss any bragging rights here, and place yourself on the scale. Where would you place yourself? Of course, in our bid to be humble, nobody that's really righteous would want to exalt themselves too much, so we cannot be too close to God. But since we are talking about goodness and righteousness, surely we would not be down close to the devil either. After all, we do some pretty good things. We might pick up the neighbor's newspaper if he's out of town or cook a meal for someone who is sick. Hey, who knows, I may even mow my neighbor's yard if it got too high, particularly the strip between his driveway and my front lawn. In fact, without bragging, and not wanting to be overly modest, I may plot myself on the Righteousness Scale at, oh, 687,132. I realize that while not right up there with God in my goodness, I'm certainly not way down next to the devil. On top of that, I'm better than the majority of people. So having plotted my righteousness well above average, I'm feeling pretty good about myself! But is that how God measures righteousness?

The problem with this kind of logic is that the entire word of God repudiates this behavior as repulsive to a holy and righteous God. We are not like God in our so-called goodness in any way. We are like other human beings, but we are not like God. There are many "good people" who strive to do their best and are kind and gracious to their fellow man. Some of these just happen to worship Allah or Buddha. Would they be considered righteous in God's eyes? Where would God place them on the scale? What about those who come knocking at your door handing out their religious path to God because they believe this earns them entrance into Heaven, would God place them higher than you on the scale? After all, when was the last time you went door-to-door handing out religious tracts? What about the person who daily seeks to do good unto others with all their heart, where might God place them on the scale? Do you see the problem? We cannot grade the righteousness of God on a scale. God is infinite in his holiness and it is impossible to quantify His righteousness. We are all so unholy when compared to God that it is easy to quantify our righteousness on a scale of one-to-a-million because we are all zeroes!

We quantify our goodness like we might quantify our golf game. I love to play golf with my son. He is a joy to watch hit the golf ball because it usually flies long and straight even in West Texas wind. My golf game is a different story entirely. My son will encourage me sometimes by saying, "Just knock it on down there, Dad!" If you are a golfer you know he's telling me to just get it as close as I can, which probably won't be very close at all.

Not long ago we were heading out to play a round of golf and I said, "Now Jordon, if I shoot this score today" – a possibly attainable score – "it will be a really good day. But Jordon, if I shoot this score" – and I hyped it up huge here with an almost impossible score to shoot – "it will be a superb day of golf. But, son if I only shoot this score" – kind of said with my head hanging down as I mention a fairly common poor score of mine – "it will just be an okay day of golf."

So there it was for me – a good day, a superb day, or just an okay day of golf. I had quantified my day so that I could measure my success. After the day was over, I'll admit that while I always have a blast playing golf with my son, my golf game itself was just another okay day of knocking it on down there and hoping to get the ball close.

As I thought about it later, I came to the conclusion that many people treat their righteousness before God in almost an exact same manner. They calculate and quantify their "acts of goodness" in such a way that if they do some good every day they will be classified as "good" by others, maybe even God. They figure if they go the extra mile and are really good, kind of like Mother Teresa or the Flying Nun or even Mary Poppins, then they are really good, maybe even superb. But if they just barely cut it, well, they're just barely acceptable in the righteousness category. Here's the problem with that kind of thinking as it relates to God – EVERYTHING!

# God's Standard of Righteousness

That is why the Gospel was such amazing, extraordinary news to the Apostle Paul. He could not be ashamed of the Gospel because he had come to the end of himself and realized that God never expected him to exhaust all of his efforts at being good. Paul realized what every person realizes if we are simply honest with ourselves. He admitted that deep down inside of all people there is something that screams our inadequacy; there is something that tells us we do not measure up, that we fall short of God's righteousness.

Romans 1:17 is such a fundamental verse in God's word as it reveals how we must define righteousness because of the sin problem that exists in all of us. This verse explains that the righteousness of God is revealed through the Gospel by faith and apart from the simple Gospel of Jesus Christ we have no hope of living a life that is pleasing to God.

This supports Isaiah's claim regarding his ill-fated attempts at personal righteousness separating him from God. Isaiah 64:6 in the New Living Translation spells out both his and our condition like this, "We are all infected and impure with sin. When we display our righteous deeds, they are nothing but filthy rags." Every act I could ever attempt on my own with the motive being to please God and earn His favor ends in failure because all of my righteous deeds are like a filthy dish rag used to wipe up my dog's vomit.

God is holy and righteous, pure and good. He exists in magnificent splendor. The angels who surround His throne proclaim His holiness without ceasing. They sing praises with glorious voices that the Creator of all is perfectly righteous and does not fit on the creations scales or standards of righteousness. The Bible teaches that God does not conform to any created standard of righteousness because...

God alone *is* the standard of righteousness.

And, as much as our pride and human logic may rebel against this idea, apart from being a Jesus follower and having our sin washed away, we are all zeroes, just like Satan, in the eyes of Almighty God, every last one of us.

## God's Definition of Righteousness

When God provided His definition of righteousness, He did so by doing the most amazing thing possible – He sent His Son. Galatians 4:4-5 speaks to this, "But when the fullness of time had come, God sent forth His Son, born of a woman, born under the law, to redeem those who were under the law, so that we might receive adoption as sons."

Every day Jesus walked this earth He displayed the righteousness of God for all to see. He walked as God. He talked as God. He displayed the works that only God can do. He painted a perfect picture of what it means to be righteous by establishing the only standard of righteousness acceptable to God the Father. He was perfect! He was the only human being to walk this earth and never sin, not even one time.

When that statement is declared, it usually is processed like high-speed internet racing through our minds and we can easily miss its great significance. Slow down to dial-up speed for a moment and process what you just read regarding Jesus never sinning. He never sinned *once*.

That declaration means that Jesus never cheated. He never stole, lied, or broke the speed limit while riding His donkey in the Jerusalem suburbs. He never manipulated others to do His will so that He might get ahead of them in the carpenter shop. The taxing authorities had no trouble with Jesus because He paid all the taxes He owed, (sometimes in very creative ways, but paid nonetheless). He never pondered thoughts that were sordid and nasty in His holy mind. Get this men, Jesus never lusted after a women, not one time. He never used "sentence enhancers" to add emphasis to His speech, (for those that don't use profanity that last statement may seem a bit confusing to you). Jesus never experienced pride, anger, envy, slothfulness, covetousness, or immorality. He never sinned! Do you see how remarkable that one thought truly is? Do you see how much this identifies Jesus as God simply because He did not do that which we all do and that is sin? Jesus lived the only perfect life, a life of total righteousness. Until the end of time Jesus has been and will forever be God's definition of righteousness for all humanity.

For those who think they may try to "wing it" and work real hard, expending all of their effort to please God apart from His Son, God's reply to them might go like this: "You want to be righteous and stand in my presence one day, mimic My Son in every detail of His life. Don't ever steal, lie, cheat, or break the speed limit. Don't ever cheat on your taxes regardless of your opinion of the Internal Revenue Service. Don't let Me catch you manipulating others for your personal gain – and of course I see everything. You'd better not think one thought that I would not approve of and that includes lusting after a person or that new designer purse that grabs your attention – and of course I know everything and can read your mind. You'd also better never let the least bit of pride, unrighteous anger, envy, slothfulness, or covetousness spring forth as a work of your hands because if you do, even one time, you will go to hell!"

When it's put like that we can easily see that it is totally and utterly impossible to make ourselves righteous and holy enough to please God and enter into His presence in eternity. No person could accomplish such an impossible task even if given 1,000 lifetimes to try as some erroneously think. We are all sinners in need of God's righteousness found only in the simple Gospel of Jesus Christ.

The divine dilemma of how to please a demanding God is what sought to drive the Augustinian Monk Martin Luther mad in 1510. Luther knew he didn't measure up to God's holy standard and had been taught all his life that he must fear God if he had any hope for a pleasant eternity. So in an effort to please God through the system of confession and penance to which he was bound, he entered the confessional almost daily, confessing every sin he could possibly think that he may have committed. He was so driven by a fear of God that he would often walk out of the confessional only to remember another sin he had forgotten, turn right around and re-enter the booth for another extended period of confession. He was ensnared by a worldly system that sought to appease an angry God by the things he was required to do rather than what Jesus had already done.

This same dilemma is seen in Paul's letter to the Philippian church where he extolls his own efforts at righteousness. Paul says, "I was circumcised when I was eight days old. I am a pure-blooded citizen of Israel and a member of the tribe of Benjamin – a real Hebrew if there ever was one! I was a member of the Pharisees, who demand the strictest obedience to the Jewish law. I was so zealous that I harshly persecuted the church. And as for righteousness, I obeyed the law without fault. I once thought these things were valuable, but now I consider them worthless because of what Christ has done. Yes, everything else is worthless when compared with the infinite value of knowing Christ Jesus my Lord. For His sake I have discarded everything else, so that I could gain Christ and become one with Him. I no longer count on my own righteousness through obeying the law; rather, I become righteous through faith in Christ. For God's way of making us right with Himself depends on faith." (Ph. 3:5-9 NLT)

Paul came to the end of himself and all his personal strivings to please God. He embraced the righteousness found only in Jesus. Paul, the great apostle, came to know that when God defined righteousness He did so through sending Jesus, the only perfect example of the standard He accepts.

## Availability

The Gospel is indeed the greatest news because it tells us that God's righteousness is personally available to all. Even in spite of the fact that we are sinners, God makes His righteousness available. Romans 3:22 says, "The righteousness of God through faith in Jesus Christ for *all* who believe." This means that righteousness not only comes totally from God but it also totally satisfies God's perfect demands. This is monumental for understanding the love of God and why even with God's coming judgment, a Jesus follower can have assurance of salvation.

When I could never satisfy or please God on my own, regardless of all of my hard work and self-effort, by placing my faith in Jesus, God's only Son, I am now acceptable to God because I am now like God. I am not a "god" myself, nor will I become one when I die as the Mormon missionary believes, but I now have the righteousness of Christ clothing me and I am declared righteous by God and will receive a wonderful, unfading inheritance from Him in eternity. Isn't that incredible? Perhaps this may help us to grab this great truth.

I remember going to my youngest daughter's high school graduation. We were so excited to watch her file into the stadium along with the hundreds of other diploma candidates. While I let out my trademark whistle to get her attention, her mother focused the telephoto lens on our baby girl to capture the moment in time. In just a short while our baby arose from her seat and filed towards the platform in anticipation of her name being called. At just the right time, her name came booming over the loud speaker and she began walking across the stage to be greeted by the school administration. When she arrived they placed in her hands a diploma and conferred upon her the title "graduate." What a picture of a before and after. When she arrived that night she was still a high school student. But just a couple of "long" hours later she was now a high school graduate.

I love this illustration because it was a great night for our family but it misses the mark in a most crucial area. While pointing to a moment in time where Raegan was declared a graduate seems to work for our illustration of being declared righteous, the fly in the ointment is that my baby girl had worked hard for the past 12 years to arrive at that moment where those in authority could declare her a graduate. That is totally contrary to our being declared righteous by God. To make this illustration work, my daughter had to unexpectedly be summoned to the school administration office where she was conferred a graduate and given a diploma. At the same time she would have had all knowledge she had worked so hard to acquire over 12 years of study infused into her instantaneously, never one time would an exam have been taken or a term paper written to measure her academic prowess. There would have been no late nights spent studying, preparing to put forth on an exam her very best the next day. Instead, all of the knowledge she actually amassed from 12 laborious, time-consuming years of hard work would have been infused as a gift right into her brain. Oh, and since we are making comparisons to God's incomparably great Gospel, why not infuse in her all of the knowledge she would have earned afterwards had she gone forth and graduated first in her class from Harvard Law? Now that's a better picture of what God does for us when He bestows upon us the righteousness of His Son. He does everything; we do nothing!

This is confirmed by one of my favorite Bible verses, 2 Corinthians 5:21. In this verse the source of our righteousness is most clearly stated, "For our sake He (God the Father) made Him (God the Son) to be sin who knew no sin, so that in Him (God the Son) we (you and I) might become the righteousness of God." So the righteousness we receive from God is totally separate from all of our self-effort because only Jesus was capable of making true righteousness available to us through His death on the cross. Only Jesus lived a perfectly sinless life, never having sinned even one time. Because of this, only Jesus could be the perfectly acceptable sacrifice so that all who believe in Him by faith could have their sins forgiven. Because of this, only by belief in Jesus does God declare any person righteous and holy in His sight. Toplady got it right when he wrote…

*Nothing in my hand I bring; simply to Thy cross I cling.*

# Ultimate Purpose

One of the reasons we fail to grasp the glory of the Gospel and why Paul is unashamed is because we do not understand God's ultimate purpose in sending forth the Gospel. We all have ideas of what God did in the Gospel, most of which are quite self-serving. We love the thought of the ultimate purpose of the Gospel being to grant us forgiveness of our sins so we can go to Heaven when we die.

In my years of ministry I have ministered to many people who have lived much of their lives pressed under the weight of guilt. It is as if they are the bright yellow daisy placed under the compounding weight of an entire set of encyclopedias to dry it out. Over time, the weight of the heavy books takes its toll on the soft pedals pressed between its pages and while the flower may be identifiable, it has lost practically all of its God-given grandeur. We are no different. Left unattended, the pressure of guilt turns a once exuberant and carefree life into a drab existence like the pressed flower. But the ultimate purpose of the Gospel is not to remove the weight of sin. It's a wonderful benefit, but not its purpose.

Perhaps you may think the ultimate purpose of the Gospel is to make you happy. After all, the Good News, if it really is good news should make us happy… right? Or maybe God gave us the Gospel to make us rich? Everybody wants to be rich and there are some Bible teachers that proclaim wealth to be available like the gold taken from Egypt when King Tut's tomb was found. Is the ultimate purpose of the Gospel to make us rich? Many in the American Church seem to think so, never stopping to think that in the eyes of the world they are rich because they live in America.

Could the ultimate purpose of the Gospel be to remove all pain and suffering that confronts us on a routine basis in life? Did God send His Son to suffer so that we might not suffer but can live every day like a new puppy rolling in the grass and chasing its tail with never a care in the world about fleas or ticks? Surely the Gospel has a greater purpose than just to take away all suffering, pain and heartache. Right?

Okay, here is what you've been waiting to hear. Surely the ultimate purpose of the Gospel must be to deliver me from hell. After all, the Bible says that God doesn't want anyone to perish and that God sent His Son so that we might have eternal life. That's it for sure; the ultimate purpose of the Gospel has to be to deliver me from hell... at least I think that's it. (Are you confused enough by now and would you like to know the answer?)

There is no question that through the Gospel we find forgiveness of our sins and for that we must be eternally thankful. We also find happiness like we've never had before once we embrace the clear teaching of the Gospel. Riches do come our way when we believe in the Gospel. Not riches according to a Wall Street standard of wealth measurement, but wealth beyond compare because of what God has in store for all of His children. Regarding the pain and suffering of this life, God never promises to deliver us from all pain and suffering on this side but rather to deliver us through every trial and hardship as He walks with us. Because of a belief in the Gospel by faith, Jesus promises to never leave us nor forsake us regardless of the intensity of the fire we find ourselves. Finally, when we accept Christ we are delivered from the gripping fear of spending an eternity separated from God in hell. No longer do we need to fear death or hell because God has a home prepared for all who trust in Him by faith. All of these are wonderful, amazing *benefits* of the Gospel, but are they the ultimate purpose of the Gospel? The answer is a resounding, "No!"

If we come to terms with how God measures righteousness, and we understand our unrighteous apart from being a Jesus follower, we can define the ultimate purpose of the Gospel as follows:

The ultimate purpose of the Gospel of Jesus Christ is to glorify God by making me, an unworthy, unholy, unrighteous, unfit person who is a zero on the one-to-a-million Righteousness Scale, *totally fit* to stand in the presence of a righteous and holy God in eternity.

God does not request I bring anything with me when I come to stand in His presence. He does not ask me to do any special work so that one day I can finally be fit to stand in His presence. No, none of these will work. So again, let's go back to the beginning of this chapter and remember some key words...

*Nothing in my hand I bring; simply to Thy cross I cling.*

Let me show you from the Bible how this works. In the Old Testament book of Zechariah, chapter 3, Joshua the high priest finds himself standing before God with Satan being present to accuse him of being unfit to be in the presence of Almighty God. Beginning in verse one, God's Word says, "Then He showed me Joshua the high priest standing before the angel of the LORD, and Satan standing at his right hand to accuse him. And the LORD said to Satan, 'The LORD rebuke you, O Satan! The LORD who has chosen Jerusalem rebuke you! Is not this a burning stick plucked from the fire?'" In other words, is Joshua the high priest not one who has been plucked from the fires of hell? The text goes on to read, "Now Joshua was standing before the angel, clothed with filthy garments. And the angel said to those who were standing before him, 'Remove the filthy garments from him.' And to him he said, 'Behold, I have taken your iniquity (sin) from you, and I will clothe you with pure vestments (garments).'" Do you see it? That is a picture of righteousness being granted once the filthiness of sin was atoned for by God. Joshua the high priest was unworthy to stand before God in his own uncleanliness. But by God's grace, Joshua's sin was taken away and then the high priest was clothed in garments fit for one who will reside in the presence of awesome holiness.

God does the same for each of us when we believe upon His Son by faith. He removes our sin by bringing us under the blood shed by Jesus on the cross so that we are cleansed. He then clothes us in the righteousness of Jesus so that when God sees us He now sees us clothed in royal robes of splendor, totally fit to stand in His royal presence.

Another passage illustrating the ultimate purpose of the Gospel is found in the sixth chapter of the Book of Isaiah. Isaiah the prophet sees the LORD high and exalted and is struck with the overwhelming knowledge that he is doomed because he is in the presence of supreme holiness. When Isaiah sees the magnificence of the Lord upon His throne and the seraphim angels circling above calling to one another, "Holy, holy, holy is the LORD of hosts; the whole earth is fully of His glory!" he realizes one thing – he is a dead man! Isaiah then confesses his filth before God, "Woe is me! For I am lost; for I am a man of unclean lips, and I dwell in the midst of a people of unclean lips; for my eyes have seen the King, the LORD of hosts!" Isaiah would have died for entering into God's presence as an unfit, unholy, and unworthy man had it not been for God immediately providing atonement for his sin. "Then one of the seraphim flew to me, having in his hand a burning coal that he had taken with tongs from the altar. And he touched my mouth and said: 'Behold, this has touched your lips; your guilt is taken away, and your sin atoned for.'" This beautiful picture in God's word reveals the inherent nature of every human being to be totally unworthy to stand in the presence of a holy God without our sins having been taken away. The coal taken from the altar is an Old Testament picture of the blood shed on the cross in the New Testament. Only through faith in Jesus, the One who shed His sinless blood at His death on the cross, dying a sacrificial death, who was buried and who was raised on the third day; only through this Jesus are our sins forgiven. Both Zechariah and Isaiah are Old Testament pictures pointing to the New Testament revealing of the ultimate purpose of the Gospel of Jesus Christ. That purpose is to take an unfit sinner like me, forgive me of my sins and clothe me in the glorious splendor of the righteousness of Jesus, for His name's sake. I bring nothing in my hands to ensure this transaction would occur, I simply believe in Jesus Christ by faith.

## Receiving God's Righteousness

The closing words of Romans 1:17 say that "the righteous shall live by faith." Paul ties down an Old Testament truth in the New Testament. That life, eternal life, comes only through faith. The New Living Translation shares Romans 1:17 in an easily understandable format, "This Good News tells us how God makes us right in His sight. This is accomplished from start to finish by faith. As the Scriptures say, 'it is through faith that a righteous person has life.'" From start to finish, to be declared righteous in the sight of God demands faith. Various translations of this verse say "from faith for faith" or "from faith to faith" or "entirely by faith" or "from faith from first to last." All of these reveal this glorious righteousness, the righteousness that makes a person fit to stand before a holy God, comes through faith alone. It's all about faith!

This is not a faith that I work myself up to believe. It is not a faith that develops as I sit in my recliner conjuring up enough faith to finally believe in the finished work of Jesus on the cross. No, like salvation, it is a faith that has been given as a gift. Ephesians chapter 2, verses 8-9 says "…by grace you have been saved through faith. And this is not your own doing; it is the gift of God, not a result of works, so that no one may boast." In other words, just as eternal life is a free gift from God, so is the faith to believe a free gift from God.

You may have never thought of the faith to believe as a free gift from God, but if you had to bring forth your own faith two things would happen. First, you would not be responding to the Gospel with empty hands, you would come carrying a faith that is your own. A faith that you have manufactured is not a true faith that has come from God. But, second, if you were able to create enough faith to earn the right to stand in the presence of a holy God, you would cease to exalt Him and would begin exalting yourself. God knows I would! If I could create, develop, or manufacture enough faith on my own to be saved, I would strut down Main Street boasting about my creation that has brought me salvation. So would you!

Let's just be honest, on our own, none of us are that faith-filled. We cannot produce enough faith to make ourselves fit to stand before a holy God in eternity, it's impossible! We are like Isaiah the prophet, and must declare "Woe is me," when confronted with the holiness of God, not "Here I am God, full of my own faith and ready to hang out with You in eternity."

So what is true believing faith? If believing faith in Jesus is not something I can produce, manufacture, conjure, or develop, what is it then? Here's the short answer to this most important question…

> True, believing faith is the *absolute rejection* of all my worthiness to be saved being totally replaced by an *absolute confidence* in the worthiness of the Lord Jesus Christ alone for salvation! Or, another way of saying it would be…
>
> *Nothing in my hand I bring; simply to Thy cross I cling.*

## The Life-Changing Power of an Empty-Handed Gospel

In 1510, the Augustinian monk Martin Luther traveled to Rome. Like many Catholics of the day he sought a pilgrimage that would draw him closer to God and shed light on many of his unanswered theological questions. While he didn't yet know it, the intense struggle he had been under as he battled internally with his divergent theology and the demands of the Roman Catholic Church were only going to increase after his fateful trip.

While in Rome he found himself kneeling at the bottom of the *Scala Sancta* or "Holy Stairs" in the Church of St. John Lateran. There he found 28 ivory stairs said to originally have been the steps leading up to Pilate's house in Jerusalem. These were steps faithful Roman Catholics believed had been trod upon by the Lord Jesus immediately before His crucifixion as He climbed them to meet with Pilate. On the stairs there were blood stains, said to have been shed by Jesus after His body had been abused badly by the Roman scourge. And there, upon those stairs, Martin Luther would make a decision that would change the course of his life and the course of history for the church.

As was tradition for all Catholic pilgrims seeking to honor God, Luther began to climb the stairs on his knees while citing prayers at each step. What he didn't realize when he mounted the stairs was that the raging battle inside of him would be played out that very day in the heart of this devout priest. The higher he crawled, the more intense the battle raged. At each step he would recognize the Catholic teaching on the fearsome wrath of God and would proclaim that the "just shall live by fear." But in almost overlapping thoughts he would find himself countering the Catholic theology deeply ingrained in his mind with the words from Romans 1:17, the "just shall live *by faith.*" No, the entirety of Catholic theology centered upon pleasing an angry God and receiving justification by fear. But then God would speak to Luther's heart, "It's not by fear, it is by faith. The just shall live *by faith.*" Slowly he ascended while the battle raged until finally Luther could stand it no more. In the middle of the *Scala Sancta* he arose and stood where he had just kneeled, no longer in fear but now in faith, fully embracing the word of God that "the just shall live by faith" in Jesus Christ alone for salvation! He was a changed man from that day forward as he embraced the Gospel of the empty hands.

*Nothing in my hand I bring; simply to Thy cross I cling.*

# chapter 5
## EVERYONE

GOSPEL CONFUSION RUNS WILD TODAY. While many remain steadfast in their understanding of the Gospel, there is a growing contingency that have dismissed the exclusivity of the Gospel for salvation. Some have abandoned the biblical teaching of a simple Gospel for the convenience of a new Gospel containing an all-inclusive salvation guaranteeing that all will be saved. Popular pastors and authors have fallen prey to the dismantling of the simple Gospel. Entire denominations have dove headlong into liberalism and are suffering the tragic consequences for their denial of the Gospel. Convenience has been chosen over truth.

Recently results were published from an inside study done by the Presbyterian Church (USA) called the "Religious and Demographic Profile of Presbyterians 2011." The findings in this comprehensive study reveal the abounding Gospel confusion of this denomination from top to bottom. One question in the study asked PCUSA pastors to define their belief in an exclusive Gospel by responding to the statement that "only followers of Jesus Christ can be saved." Upon doing so an astounding 45% disagreed or strongly disagreed with this statement. Only 41% of the PCUSA pastors confessed to agreement or strong agreement that Jesus is the only way to eternal life. These results not only support Gospel confusion, it vividly reflects this denomination's Gospel denial!

One responder in the comment stream offered the following insider's viewpoint. Calling himself "PresbyMike" he says, "This is my tribe and none of this surprises me. We have tried every spiritual and theological fad of the last 50 years except for an exuberant orthodoxy. Sadly, this is probably the least likely response we will take to head off our demise. Unlike the church of Ephesus in Revelation 2, Jesus doesn't have to remove our lampstand. We are already doing it for Him."[3]

As we've seen, the Bible is clear that all have sinned and that the wages of sin is death. Since all have sinned and are spiritually dead before Jesus rescues them, everyone is unquestionably in need of the Gospel.

By this time, we are well acquainted with the Gospel and know that it means "good news." It is the good news that Jesus died, was buried, and raised to life on the first Easter morning and that all that call on Him alone for salvation can and will be saved. That's good news!

The goal of this chapter is to explain that the Gospel is available for everyone. It is not for an exclusive few; it is good news that salvation is available to all who call upon the name of Jesus for salvation.

Paul says in Romans 1:16 and 17, "For I am not ashamed of the Gospel, for it is the power of God for salvation to *everyone* who believes, to the Jew first and also to the Greek. For in [the Gospel] the righteousness of God is revealed from faith for faith, as it is written, 'The righteous shall live by faith.'"

The simple Gospel of Jesus is good news! Paul was unashamed to inscribe these words we've just read on parchment because he'd dramatically encountered the good news of the Gospel. With that in mind, I want to elaborate for a moment on this truth:

The Gospel is only good news because it is available for everyone!

If the Gospel were exclusive to people of a certain race, gender, religious denomination or social status, it would be good news only until someone we love falls outside those exclusive boundaries. For example, if the Gospel ruled out people on the basis of their geographic location, there would be no need for mission teams to travel to Oman, Bahrain, India or China. Or, perhaps we would be the ones excluded from salvation, imagine that? In our egocentrism in the West, we would all assume the Gospel is for us and would feel quite content in believing this as God's sovereign will to save only those living where we live. We know that logic is flawed.

---

3   Jeff Gissing, *The Coming Collapse of the PC(USA),* See Article and Comment Stream at *http://juicyecumenism.com/2013/07/24/the-coming-collapse-of-the-pc-usa/*.

If the Gospel were linked to an upper crust social status, as long as we were members in good standing at the local country club we could feel good about eternity. If the Gospel was available to only a certain skin color, a preferred race of people if you will, we could breathe a sigh of relief if our skin pigment fit the prescribed salvation boundaries. How ridiculous!

For the Gospel to be God's great, good news, it must be *available* to everyone. Those who disagree with this thought, do not struggle with the sovereignty of God, they struggle with the salvation plan of God.

Missionary-minded Paul must have been aflame when the Holy Spirit inspired him to write, "For I am not ashamed of the Gospel for it is the power of God for salvation to *everyone* who believes, to the Jew first and also to the Greek." Here Paul is not establishing a religious pecking order for entrance into heaven nearly as much as he is denoting a chronological unveiling of God's plan.

The Gospel entered the world through the Jewish people. The Son of God was Jewish. He came as Deliverer and Messiah, as the Savior. He alone presents the way to eternal life and His message was first preached to the Jews and then to the Gentile world. It was the plan of God to include gentiles for salvation all along. For this reason, when the Jews rejected Jesus, the door was opened for Gospel-preaching missionaries to spread the good news that salvation is available to everyone who believes. As I said, the inclusion of Gentiles into God's plan for eternity was not an afterthought of God. When you study the Bible from Genesis forward you find God often speaks of the Gentile nations coming into His Kingdom. When you arrive at the New Testament, you hear the invitation not just offered to Jews, but the offer of salvation to everyone comes directly from the mouth of Jesus.

Throughout the remainder of the New Testament you find this great Gospel offered as a free gift to all who will believe. God has done this for His glory. He desires countless numbers of His creation, of every color and social status to worship Him in eternity. He will be worshiped by a multitude rather than an exclusive few in Heaven. Revelation 7:9 contains my favorite picture of Heaven, "After this I looked, and behold, a great multitude that no one could number, from every nation, from all tribes and peoples and languages, standing before the throne and before the Lamb." What a spectacular time of worship!

# Jesus and "Whoever"

I said a moment ago that Jesus offered salvation to everyone He encountered. Let's take a moment and look only in the Gospel of John at some of the many references spoken by Jesus to prove the point that the Gospel is available for whoever will call out to God by faith in His Son. Check out these verses from the English Standard Version of the Bible:

- John 3:15 – "...*whoever* believes in Him (Jesus) may have eternal life."

- John 3:16 – "For God so love the world, that He gave His only Son, that *whoever* believes in Him should not perish but have eternal life."

- John 3:18 – "*Whoever* believes in Him (Jesus) is not condemned, but *whoever* does not believe is condemned already, because he has not believed in the name of the only Son of God."

- John 3:36 – "*Whoever* believes in the Son has eternal life; *whoever* does not obey the Son shall not see life, but the wrath of God remains on him."

- John 4:14 – "But *whoever* drinks of the water that I (Jesus) will give him will never be thirsty again."

- John 5:24 – "Truly, truly, I say to you, *whoever* hears my word and believes Him who sent me has eternal life. He does not come into judgment, but has passed from death to life."

- John 6:40 – "For this is the will of my Father, that *everyone* who looks on the Son and believes in Him should have eternal life, and I will raise him up on the last day."

- John 6:47 – "Truly, truly, I say to you, *whoever* believes has eternal life."

- John 7:38 – "*Whoever* believes in me, as the Scripture has said, 'Out of his heart will flow rivers of living water.'"

- John 8:12 – "Again Jesus spoke to them, saying, 'I am the light of the world. *Whoever* follows me will not walk in darkness, but will have the light of life.'"

- John 11:25 and 26 – "Jesus said to her, 'I am the resurrection and the life. *Whoever* believes in me, though he die, yet shall he live, and *everyone* who lives and believes in me shall never die. Do you believe this?'"

Do you think it's possible that Jesus is making a point through redundancy? Could He be any more explicit that the Gospel is good news because it is available to whoever calls upon His name for salvation? Wouldn't you agree with that? Jesus is saying that the Gospel is available for *everyone*!

There are many other references in the New Testament that support this claim. One piece of evidence is found in Acts chapter 2. In verse 21, Peter draws the net in his sermon by quoting the Old Testament prophet Joel, "And it shall come to pass that everyone who calls upon the name of the Lord shall be saved."

The same theme runs through the remainder of the Bible. In Revelation, the last book in the Bible, in chapter 22, the last chapter in the Bible, in the fourth from the last verse in the Bible, a final invitation is given, guaranteeing the Gospel is available for everyone. Verse 17 in the New International Version says, "The Spirit and the bride say, 'Come!' And let him who hears say, 'Come!' *Whoever* is thirsty, let him come; and *whoever* wishes, let him take the free gift of the water of life." There it is ... *whoever* ... *whoever*. The Gospel is good news because, and only because, it is available for everyone!

So when Paul says that the Gospel "is the power of God for salvation to *everyone* who believes, to the Jew first and also to the Greek" he provides no qualifiers such as race, color or geography. Faith in the Son is the only divine dividing wall for salvation. The Gospel is available for any person on the face of the earth who calls upon the name of Jesus Christ. That is incredible news!

# Jesus Followers

I've used the term "Jesus follower" numerous times in this book already. Many of you holding this book would describe yourself as a Jesus follower. You have accepted His great offer of salvation. The simple Gospel has become real to you. It could have happened when you were five or seventy-five. You came to a moment in your life where you recognized an unmet spiritual need you could no longer dismiss. Without even realizing the power of the Holy Spirit of God at work, you admitted that you were a sinner in need of God's forgiveness. Just as if you and He were sitting in a room together and you heard him whisper your name, you turned your face toward God and believed the Gospel. At that moment, before you were baptized or confirmed or attended a Discovery Class, you became a believer in Jesus, a Jesus follower.

It happened in my daughter Avery's life when she was five. She was riding with her mother to a Bible study Andi was attending at our church in Houston. On the short journey there, Andi had tuned into a local Christian radio station where Pastor David Lino was presenting the Gospel. All of a sudden, our little Avery began to cry huge tears of brokenness. Being the great mom she is, Andi turned the radio off and asked Avery what was wrong. Without hesitation Avery cried through her emotion, "I'm a sinner Mommy, I'm a sinner! I've done sins!" Andi found a place to park and asked Avery why she felt this way. Our baby went on to explain that she had taken some make-up out of her mommy's closet and she now knew this was a sin. She was very clear on the truth that she was a sinner in need of forgiveness and she was only five. Andi explained that God had provided a way for our sins to be forgiven through the death of Jesus on the cross. She placed the Gospel before our 5-year-old daughter and told her the good news that her sins could be washed away and she could receive forgiveness for stealing make-up and for every other sin she had committed or would ever commit. And there, in the quietness of our old, red van, Heaven came down as Avery received the forgiveness of God by believing the Gospel. At that moment, she became a Jesus follower.

One Good Friday afternoon while our kids were hunting Easter eggs, I stood on the parking lot of the local Methodist church and visited with a friend of mine named Troy. He was a hardworking man who hauled heavy equipment from location to location to support the East Texas logging industry. Troy explained to me that his interest in salvation had been pricked because of a funeral he had attended that I officiated. I knew better. It wasn't my sermon that brought about Troy and my visit. His interest was piqued because the Holy Spirit was drawing him to become a Jesus follower. As we stood there on that Friday, Troy acknowledged he was a sinner and believed upon Jesus for the first time in his life. On that day, Troy became a Jesus follower.

In 2004, my family was relocating from a place we adored to the other side of the state. We were excited for the new adventure but sad to leave where we had planted our hearts. There were many unknowns, but God was directing our move. Before I packed my office I had a church member named Pete stop in for a visit. He had the look of a cowboy, around 70 years old. I never saw Pete when he didn't have a smile on his face. We'd first met when I became pastor of the church he and his family faithfully attended. He was present on most Sundays and also attended numerous Bible studies I'd taught. On this particular day, however, Pete was burdened. He sat in my office with tears in his eyes because he'd known for a long time that something was missing inside. We visited for a while and then got down on our knees together. Pete confessed and truly believed. On that day, Pete became a Jesus follower.

There are many stories such as these I could tell, but all of them would have the same common factors. Each person, regardless of age, realized they were a sinner, and that they had sinned personally. They understood their sin was against God and also recognized their need for forgiveness. Each one confessed their sin and turned to Jesus, believing in the completed work He did on the cross in their place. In other words, they heard and understood the simple Gospel that is available only through Jesus. On that particular day, when they placed their faith in the Son of God alone, they received forgiveness and eternal life. They became Jesus followers and proved the Gospel is for everyone. But, is this almost *too good* to be true?

## Too Good to be True

We hear advertisements that are too good to be true all the time. I was driving in Dallas one day, pulled up to a red light and noticed a small hand-written sign stuck beside the road. It read, "Salesmen needed $28K monthly!" Now that's too good to be true! What legitimate company where the sales people can earn $28,000 monthly advertises with a yard sign next to a busy intersection. I'm not that gullible. I know that's too good to be true and I'm not buying it!

Somewhat like that yard sign, there are those who view the Gospel as false advertising, just too good to be true. They reject it out of hand as impossible. Because there are so many "swindlers" today, we need a proper measure of skepticism, even in religious circles. But to dismiss the Gospel as false advertising and too good to be true is a hasty decision for sure. Some things that sound impossible really prove to be just the opposite.

What if I told you that it was possible to take one tiny red paper clip and barter it away for an entire two-story house, would you believe me? Perhaps you would if I've proven myself to be trustworthy and a man of integrity. However, you would probably have your doubts and say that you're not that gullible because my logic sounds totally too good to be true. The thought that anyone could take a red paper clip worth only a few cents and trade it for a house worth thousands is outrageous.

Let me introduce you to Canadian Kyle McDonald. In 2005, all he had of value was one red paper clip. He thought, "What could I do with one red paper clip?" Kyle was familiar with Craig's List and how it worked so he understood the game of bartering. One day he posted on Craig's List his idea, "I want to trade one red paper clip for something. What would you give me for it?" Just a few days later, some girls in another part of Canada saw his listing. They called him on the telephone and said, "Hi Kyle, we'll trade you a really unique pen, a writing pen shaped like a fish for your one red paper clip." Shortly they met in front of a convenience store, took a quick picture to record the start of something epic, and made the swap. Kyle traded his one red paper clip for their unique fish-shaped writing pen. He then posts on Craig's List that he has a fish-shaped writing pen he would like to trade. Soon, he trades the pen for a little doorknob with a smiley face on it. From there the trades continue with Kyle's bartering plan mushrooming into something big. Just 14 trades later he makes his final trade for a house in Saskatchewan, Canada for *free*. He began with one little red paper clip.[4]

I share this to prove that what seems impossible and too good to be true shouldn't always be dismissed sight unseen. If an ingenious man can do

---

4   You can read the full story at http://oneredpaperclip.com.

the seemingly impossible and barter away one red paper clip for a beautiful house, can't the God of all creation do much, much more to defy the appearance of impossibility? While the offer of forgiveness of sin and eternal life seems impossible because it is totally free, let's not reject it without first understanding what we are saying is too good to be true. Agreed?

Let's not become so jaded that we can't believe what's true. Let's not become so skeptical that we doubt and dismiss everything new that comes along that doesn't fit inside our perfectly defined box. I say this because when God gave us the Gospel, it was most assuredly outside the box of normal thinking! Even when the Bible was written, there were those who stood in judgment of the Gospel saying, "No way, this isn't gonna work! It's too good to be true! There's no way this is from God! Besides, Jesus was executed with criminals on a Roman cross!" In 1 Corinthians 1:18 in the New Living Translation the Bible says, "The message of the cross is foolish to those who are headed to destruction but we who are being saved know that it is the very power of God." There will be those who will not accept the Gospel because they are going to say it's too good to be true. I hope that's not you. God offers an overcoming life to all who simply believe in that which *appears* too good to be true... the Gospel.

## World's Greatest Equalizer

Because the Gospel is available for everyone, it is the greatest equalizer the world has ever known. We live in a society that loves the uncommon, the exclusive. Advertisers who sell high-end products to wealthy customers use this as their primary marketing strategy. Even in lower to middle income groups people still enjoy finding that which is rare and unusual.

My mother takes antique shopping to a whole new level. Every vacation when I was a child we always had time carved into our schedule for stopping by little roadside antique shops. To this day my mom can spot an antique bargain from 40 paces. It's almost like she has an innate sense that there is something exclusive and exceptional just ahead if she will just pull the car in for a brief, or not so brief, look around.

I was digging around on the internet for exclusive "things" recently and I found the most expensive hotel on the planet for a one night stay. According to the internet, the Hotel President Wilson in Geneva, Switzerland wins the prize for most exclusive with that one night stay totaling a mere $65,000.00. Pretty exclusive, wouldn't you think?

We appreciate rare paintings, and rare treasures like diamonds and other precious gems. If you examine the list of the ten most expensive diamonds on earth, you'll find the 45.52 caret Hope diamond worth over $350,000,000 at number four on the list. Item number one is owned by the British Crown Jewels and cannot be valued because of its exclusivity.

I share all of this to prove the exceptional treasure we have in the Gospel. The simple Gospel of Jesus Christ is of far more worth than a one night stay in Switzerland or even the entire list of the world's rarest diamonds. Yet it is not so exclusive that anybody ever need say, "I could never have that." It is not so costly that anyone would ever say, "I could never afford that." The truth is that the Gospel is so very exclusive that no person on earth has enough wealth or prestige to purchase or merit receiving it. But God says to everyone, "Here's a free gift of inestimable value that I want to give you. And not just to you only, I will make it available to everyone who will call upon the name of my Son." That is what He's talking about. The Gospel is the greatest equalizer because it is available from God to every person on the face of the earth.

A man, who sleeps in his ragged clothes every night, only to awaken on the streets the next morning to beg for money, stands at the foot of the cross just like the wealthiest billionaire in America. They will both arrive at the same spot at the foot of the cross through a poverty of spirit or they will not be received. In Matthew 5:3, Jesus said, "Blessed are the poor in spirit, for theirs is the kingdom of Heaven."

In the same way, the person who works in the rapid fire environment of Wall Street and wears Brooks Brothers and Armani daily will stand before the cross of Jesus no differently than a country girl who goes to work at Wal-Mart making minimum wage to help feed her family and make ends meet.

Both have the same salvation available to them through Jesus. Whether you are a doctor, lawyer, accountant or engineer, it doesn't matter because you can flip the coin over and say that those who have nothing can have everything through Jesus Christ. The Gospel is without question the greatest equalizer the world has ever known.

God looks at no person and gives them special privileges. He never says, "Because of who *you* are I'm going to get you a better deal than all the rest." There are no plan upgrades because the deluxe package comes to every person as a free gift from God. Just take it. It's a free gift. You believe upon Jesus. It's a free gift.

Acts chapter 2 explains this in a wonderful way. This chapter relates the coming of the Holy Spirit upon the 120 Jesus followers on the Day of Pentecost. Verse 4 says, "And they were all filled with the Holy Spirit and began to speak in other tongues (other languages) as the Spirit gave them utterance." When the power of the Holy Spirit came upon these first believers, they began speaking in different languages and the people standing nearby heard them and were amazed!

In verse 8 of Acts 2 the Bible says, "And how is it that we hear, each of us in his own native language?" And then look at how many different languages were being spoken on that day. Acts 2:9-11, "Parthians and Medes and Elamites and residents of Mesopotamia, Judea and Cappadocia, Pontus and Asia, Phrygia and Pamphylia, Egypt and the parts of Libya belonging to Cyrene, and visitors from Rome, both Jews and proselytes, Cretans and Arabians – we hear them telling in our own tongues the mighty works of God." There are 16 different names or people groups listed in these verses. That is 16 different groups containing Jews and proselytes who were now told of one common factor available to all. When Peter preached his sermon that day, 16 different groups were hearing that the Gospel is available to them if they but call upon the name of Jesus Christ. The Gospel has no regard for what tribe or region of the world you reside. It is available to all people everywhere!

It says: "…that all were amazed and perplexed, 'what does this mean?'" It means that the Gospel is the greatest equalizer that the world has ever known. God does not look at geographical regions or prosperity profiles. He does not look at the door number on our houses and arbitrarily select those with even numbers to be saved. God sent Jesus Christ to die for all who would believe on Him and receive eternal life. That's incredible news.

## Raising the Stakes

Because the Gospel is available for everyone, it elevates human responsibility to eternal proportion. The more I study and meditate upon verse 16, "For I am not ashamed of the Gospel," the greater my belief that Paul is overcome with joy because he has benefited directly. He is a verbal witness to the goodness and grace of God. "For I am not ashamed of the Gospel, for it is the power of God for salvation to everyone," he says, "who believes."

The stakes are raised because when you hear the Gospel message, you are immediately charged with a decision that takes on eternal proportions. Human responsibility kicks in and demands something be done with what has been heard. We are responsible to do something with the Gospel. To turn our backs on the special gift of the Gospel is utterly ridiculous. To look the other way when we see people in need of the Gospel is an offense to God.

Years ago an African missionary was taking a group of short-term volunteers to a remote village to share the Gospel. On the first morning as they drove down the wild and winding dirt road towards the village, the car was infused with excitement. The volunteers were getting their first taste of Africa and were boots on the ground for Jesus and couldn't wait to share the good news with those in desperate need to hear. Before they drove around the final bend in the road and entered the village, the wise missionary brought the car to a stop. "Why are we stopping?" was the question fired his way. Here is the missionary's response: "I want you to understand what you are about to do. When you arrive in this village you will see and feel a spiritual darkness more real than you've ever experienced. I have stopped the car because the moment we go around the bend ahead and you see this village, you are responsible before God to do something about what you've just witnessed." The light-hearted mood suddenly changed as each person grasped the human responsibility before them to share God's good news.

The stakes are raised in thousands of bible-believing churches around the world every Sunday when a faithful pastor stands and declares truth from God's word regarding the Gospel. On so many occasions I have had people come to me after a particularly moving sermon and say something like this, "Pastor, when you preached that message last week on the Gospel, I still can't believe somebody didn't get saved. Oh, pastor, you just keep being encouraged, okay? Don't get down that nobody got saved. Be encouraged." I know these dear people are trying to encourage me so my response will usually be, "Thank you so much for encouraging me and please continue to pray that when the Gospel goes forth, people will respond."

However, this is what I've learned through many years of ministry. Long ago, I learned that God has called me to provide the best, absolute best, outward presentation of the Gospel I possibly can by His power and grace. That's my calling when I preach. After that, I'm charged with one other thing… I must leave the results to Him!

There are some communicators of the Word of God who think they are something more than a delivery boy, or a mouthpiece. They are not! I have never saved any person. I do not have the power to save anyone. Jesus is the Savior. He is the one who saves all who will be saved. Any person who hears the Gospel message and delays becoming a Jesus follower is walking a tightrope headed to hell. If you utilize the human responsibility you have been given by God to reject His Son, you will fall from the tightrope one day and will wonder for eternity, "Oh my God, why did I not listen when the pastor was speaking and why did I not receive Jesus Christ then?" The same will happen to every person reading these words as only an academic exercise but you have no desire to believe in Jesus and be saved. You're going to remember what you are reading right now when you get to hell. My prayer for you is that you would not reject the Gospel but would embrace that it is available to you at this very moment.

You ask, "What should my response be?" It should be the same as those who heard Peter's anointed sermon that day so many years ago. Acts 2:37 spells out the initial reaction to hearing the Gospel, "Now when they heard this they were cut to the heart." They were convicted to respond to the Gospel not by Peter but by the Holy Spirit because the Gospel is "the power of God for salvation," not the power of Peter. Verse 37 goes on to say, "they were cut to the heart, and said to Peter and the rest of the apostles, 'Brothers, what shall we do?'" They recognized they were responsible for what they had just heard. They just didn't know how to exercise their newly recognized responsibility.

"Brothers, what shall we do?" That's a great question, the question of human responsibility. *What shall we do?* Verses 38-39 give us Peter's answer. "And Peter said to them, 'Repent and be baptized every one of you [again the Gospel for *everyone*] in the name of Jesus Christ for the forgiveness of your sins, and you will receive the gift of the Holy Spirit. For the promise is for you and for your children and for all who are far off, everyone whom the Lord our God calls to Himself." The Gospel is available for *everyone*, Peter says.

I realize many today desire to debate how God calls someone to salvation. When I preach, every time I share the Gospel it is an outward call to respond and embrace what has just been stated. If you are reading this, the call of the Gospel has been made to you. It is available to everyone, what they do with what they have heard falls upon their shoulders.

So remember, the Gospel is God's call to become a Jesus follower to every person who hears this call. If it were not so, it would not be good news. The Gospel is good news because it is available for everyone. If it were available for just a few, that's not good news to me nor is it good news for you either. Unless, perhaps you could somehow prove you were one of the elect apart from Scripture and that would be impossible.

# Pay it Forward

Because the Gospel is available for everyone, it obligates every Jesus follower to join in the task of paying the good news forward to others. The need for us to tell others the good news we've heard is urgent. If we look again at Romans 1:14, we gain a sense of Paul's urgency and his obligation. This verse says, "I am under *obligation* both to Greeks and to barbarians, both to the wise and to the foolish." In other words, he is saying that, "I am under obligation to everyone I encounter to tell them about Jesus Christ, to pay forward the good news I've heard and received." He goes on to say in verse 15, "So I am eager to preach the Gospel to you also who are in Rome." Paul's obligation to preach the Gospel leads him to a profound eagerness to finish the task.

By its very nature, the Gospel demands to be paid forward by everyone who declares themselves a Jesus follower. We are under extreme obligation to God to take seriously this responsibility. Here's how we arrive at this most important obligation.

Paul first saw himself under obligation to God because God had called him to preach the Gospel to the Gentile nation. The Bible says in 1 Corinthians 9:16, "Woe to me if I do not preach the Gospel!" So we understand Paul's obligation to God and His Gospel. But take it one step further. Paul is also obligated, he says, to the Greeks and to the barbarians, the wise and the unwise. In its sweetest essence, Paul sees himself under obligation to share the Gospel with every person whenever possible because he's got good news that they can receive the same salvation he has received. That's why he is burdened with this intense obligation to preach the good news.

Perhaps an example of the burden we carry to pay forward the Gospel can be seen in this: If I am walking down the road and I see a house on fire,

I have an obligation to do what I can to alert others that a house is burning. At the very least, I am obligated to alert the fire department and other rescue personnel. I have a moral responsibility to society to render aid by at least calling 9-1-1. Do I not? If I hear a child crying inside the burning house, I have an obligation to do all I can to reach that child before the flames. In much the same way, if I am standing at a window looking at my neighbor's beautiful swimming pool and I see a toddler tumble into the pool, I have a moral obligation to react and do something. To attempt no rescue and notify no person that the baby is drowning makes me guilty of the death of the child. While nobody may ever know what I have witnessed, God knows and sees! Or, if I'm walking with you in the cool evening and you fall to the ground having a heart attack, I'm under obligation to do something, right? If we are fishing and you step off into quicksand and can't get yourself out, do I have an obligation to help you get out? Of course I do! You are in danger of dying and I have a very real obligation to do all that I can to render aid.

On September 19, 2013 my father-in-law was living in our home for health reasons. He was growing stronger daily, but on this particular night God had other plans. While a commercial break stopped play of the football game he and I were watching, I ran upstairs to check on some things while he stepped out onto our back porch. In a couple of minutes I heard him knocking to get into the house. He'd locked himself out. Seconds after I opened the door he fell into the chair he'd been sitting on having what we later learned was most likely cardiac arrest. In seconds, my wife called 9-1-1 and I began CPR. The ambulance arrived in 10 minutes and took him to the emergency room. They did all they could to save this man they'd never met but he was pronounced dead a short while later. I share this with you for this reason. Had we just stood there scratching our head and watching him pass into eternity, it would have been both unloving and irresponsible. But because we acted and did everything within our powers to assist one we loved so dearly, we are comforted. We had a responsibility and obligation to render aid but God in His sovereignty desired my father-in-law to be in Heaven.

When analyzing our moral responsibilities to pay forward the Gospel to others, do you think we have little or no obligation to those walking into a Christ-less eternity in hell? Do we just watch them go to hell, scratch our head and do nothing about it? We should be ashamed if that is what we believe! Every Jesus follower has an obligation placed upon them by God and His Word to pay forward our salvation just like Paul and seek to help as many as possible go to heaven before they breathe their last.

We know the Great Commission; I've given it to you earlier but it bears repeating. Jesus said in Matthew 28:18-20, "And Jesus came and said to them, 'All authority in heaven and on earth has been given to Me. Go therefore, and make disciples of all nations, baptizing them in the Father and of the Son and of the Holy Spirit, teaching them to observe all that I have commanded you. And behold, I am with you always, to the end of the age." Does that not speak to the obligation of every Jesus follower to pay forward the Gospel?

Acts chapter 1, verse 8, are the last words we have from our Lord before He ascended into Heaven. He says, "But you will receive power when the Holy Spirit comes on you and you will be my witnesses in Jerusalem and all Judea and Samaria and to the end of the earth." We have an obligation to be His witnesses.

When I was a little boy, there was a popular television show called "Lassie." Most of you don't remember Lassie, but she was cool with a capital "C" to say the least. Lassie's owner was little Timmy. Little Timmy often found himself in trouble, regularly putting his life in danger. But never fear; Lassie was the smartest dog on television. She gave every appearance as a canine of having mastered much of the English language. This of course paid dividends every time little Timmy would hurt himself or fall into a ravine and be unable to get out. At the most desperate moment, Timmy would cry out in his little voice for help to his trusted best friend, "Lassie! Lassie! Go find me help, girl!" Lassie would stand there for a second, cock her head to convey understanding, give a doggie nod and a "Woof!" and off she would go to get help. She would run up to little Timmy's house and stand outside barking until someone responded. When Timmy's parents walked onto the front porch, able to understand canine as well as Lassie could English, they would say, "What is it Lassie? Where is Timmy, he must be hurt? Oh, we've not a moment to lose, little Timmy is hurt!" I pray to God that Lassie is not a better witness than we. I pray that a dog is not better at paying forward a good deed than the Church in America. I'm quite serious when I say this because all around us we meet people in trouble. People who are messed up by life and unable to save themselves. What are we going to do? The Gospel is available for everyone and it is a mandate from God that we play our part in paying forward this great Gospel with the same eagerness as the Apostle Paul because lostness is everywhere.

# chapter 6
## "I HAVE SPIT ON THE GROUND!"

THERE IS NOTHING LIKE THE Gospel of Jesus Christ and nothing can compare to it. It is the greatest news on the face of the earth. It is the news we are privileged to share with others. It is the wonderful news that Jesus is alive and He wants to have a personal relationship with us.

Since Jesus followers have been summoned to share the Gospel with others, the Gospel is very much a call to action. It is a divine mandate to fully engage in the most important work on earth – making Jesus known to those who do not know Him yet! It is a call we must take seriously.

I am privileged to serve as a trustee with the International Mission Board (IMB) of the Southern Baptist Convention. At our quarterly meetings we enjoy fellowship with other trustees and the staff of this large mission sending agency. The highlight of each two-day meeting is hearing from the president of the IMB, Tom Elliff. Recently Tom shared a story of a visit he'd had with his dear friend and former Senior Vice President of the IMB, Avery Willis. It seems Avery had introduced a young Muslim to faith in Jesus Christ. Knowing the high cost and even danger that comes with making such a claim in the Middle East, where tolerance of Christianity is quite nonexistent, Avery sought to help the young fellow count the cost of the decision he'd made. As he told of the coming hardships, the Muslim boy turned Jesus follower looked into the eyes of Willis and said, "I have spit on the ground; I will not lick it up!"

What a graphic illustration used to evidence the young boy's resolve to follow Jesus. Come what may, this boy was stepping outside of his comfort zone and surrendering his life to Jesus. "I have spit on the ground; I will not lick it up!" What a challenge to those of us who *do not* face trials and persecution simply because we have turned our eyes towards Jesus. Do we hold a similar conviction as this boy?

Are you prepared to make a resolute statement of that magnitude regarding your faith as a Jesus follower? Would you be willing to say, "I have heard and believed the Gospel and have spit on the ground; I will not lick it up. I have made my decision, and the decision is final. Whatever happens to me, I accept. I have spit on the ground and I will not lick it up."

That is the only level of commitment truly acceptable to God. Regardless of whether you live in Houston, New York, Paris, or Saudi Arabia, because of the great, good news of the Gospel, you should be like that Muslim turned Jesus follower in your devotion. God demands this from all followers, not just from a Muslim boy living seven thousand miles away from America.

When we take the Gospel seriously, we must always take it as a call to action. Everywhere Jesus went, He preached the Gospel. His sermons were heavy with application because He expected those who heard to do something with the knowledge they had now gained. He preached so that people would respond by making a decision. He preached for action!

It's no different today. The Gospel is a call to get out of our comfort zones, shift from neutral to drive, and move forward. It is a call to hard work.

On several occasions West Texas oil tycoon, Clayton Williams and I have visited about life. I'll admit to being intrigued by the business acumen of this old cowboy. He has made fortunes, lost them, and made even more digging in the dirt for black gold. One day, my son and I were talking to Clayton and he told us the ultimate secret to getting ahead. Everything got quiet and we stood still. When someone as successful as Clayton speaks about business success, wise people listen. With great interest I looked him in the eye and asked if he'd let the two of us in on his secret. He said, "Why sure I will, it's real easy. The secret is to keep your head down and your 'bottom' up and work!"

That's the attitude that has made him a vast fortune drilling for oil. It is also the attitude that every Jesus follower should have when it comes to our determination to mine this world sharing the Gospel as we go. Heads down!

## Cotton Fields at Harvest Time

I had never seen cotton fields ready to be harvested until we moved to West Texas. It's easy to see when it's time to pick the cotton because the field is totally white with beautiful, puffy cotton having burst forth from the bowl. Every time I drive by a field like this, the words of Jesus in John 4, verse 35 come alive. He says, "Look, I tell you, lift up your eyes, and see that the fields are white for harvest." For every generation, the fields are still white and the harvest is still needed. The question we must answer is this: Are we so moved and enthralled with this great Gospel we have received that we are willing to go into those fields and participate in the harvest God has planned?

Jesus also uses harvest imagery in Matthew chapter 9, verses 35 to 38, "And Jesus went throughout all the cities and villages, teaching in their synagogues and proclaiming the Gospel of the Kingdom and healing every disease and every affliction. When He saw the crowds, He had compassion for them, because they were harassed and helpless, like sheep without a shepherd. Then He said to His disciples, 'The harvest is plentiful but the laborers are few. Therefore, pray earnestly to the Lord of the harvest to send out laborers into His harvest.'"

The Gospel deserves our firm resolve to take seriously the words of Jesus we've just read. This is the heartbeat of missions and evangelism, taking seriously the words of Jesus and moving into the harvest fields. It demands and deserves our total resolve to accomplish the task.

## Resolved

The Lord Jesus is going from town to town preaching in the synagogues, on the hillside and in the streets. Wherever He goes, He's preaching the Gospel. You may wonder, "If the Gospel is the good news of the death, burial and resurrection of Jesus, how is Jesus preaching the Gospel?" Good question. The answer is that Jesus is the embodiment of the good news. He is the living, breathing, flesh on bones embodiment of the Gospel. Every time He opened His mouth to teach and help people break free from their religious bondage, the Lord Jesus Christ was preaching the good news. He was telling them how they could be set free, how the chains could come off. He was most definitely preaching good news! Jesus preached the Gospel better than any person who has ever lived. Of course we know this to be true because He alone is the Son of God. But also, Jesus had a unique view of the world to which He preached.

## How Jesus Views the World

Have you ever paused to learn how Jesus views the world? What did He see 2,000 years ago and would He view the world the same if He walked on earth today? If we can look at the world through the eyes of Jesus, we can better understand the resolution we make to stand firm for His Gospel.

As I write, a civil war is boiling in Syria. There have been millions of Syrian Muslims displaced from their homes. Millions of children have fled with their parents and are staying in refugee camps. We've seen similarly heartbreaking stories come from other countries around the world. What does Jesus think when He looks from Heaven and sees the killing and chaos?

What does Jesus think when He sees the religious frenzy going on in Egypt at this time? What does He think when Muslim religious extremists are burning Christian churches and destroying any semblance of a democratic government? What does Jesus think?

What does He think when He looks down at the city where you live? I ask this question about Odessa, what does Jesus think about Odessa, Texas at this moment in time? There are no wars going on in Odessa. My friends and family live in relative peace and quiet. But what does Jesus think about daily life in Odessa or in your hometown? Frankly, I would bet a dollar to a donut, as my cousin used to say, that Jesus looks at the world today – whether Syria, Egypt, or Odessa – just as He looked at the world 2,000 years ago. Let's find out.

## Harassed People

When Jesus walked among the people in Galilee, He saw a world full of harassed people. Verse 36 says he was filed with compassion "because they were harassed." Jesus saw a weary group of people, people fighting to survive every single day. They awoke in the morning and went about their daily life harassed by the activities of the world. It was not a once in a while harassment, it was trouble every single day as they lived with unseen spiritual forces around them seeking to keep them enchained to the ritualistic life of worthless religion.

What I have just described is the job description Satan gives to his minions every day, to harass people so they keep their eyes looking down rather than up toward God? You wonder why you have trouble some days, it's because a demonic team of "harassment experts" have gotten your number and their sole goal is to cause you problems. They are harassing you!

When Jesus preached the Gospel, Satan was lurking in the shadows hoping to steal the words Jesus spoke and keep the masses blinded to the truth? Satan doesn't want any person to see the truth of the Gospel! He is a hard worker, striving diligently with his head down and his bottom up to blind the mind of unbelievers today.

That's what the Word of God says in 2 Corinthians 4:4, "...the god of this world has blinded the minds of the unbelievers to keep them from seeing the light of the Gospel of the glory of Christ, who is the image of God." Jesus looks down even today and He sees people who are harassed and blinded by Satan.

## Helpless

Jesus traveled about preaching to people He knew to be helpless to fix their problems. You might ask, "Helpless to fix *what* problems?" They were helpless to help themselves. They could not fix their broken spiritual condition on their own. They would try to please God with their acts of service, but the bondage they felt only lead to increased helpless feelings.

Jesus sees people today sprinting headlong in their pursuit of false religions that make promises He knows cannot be kept. He watches people seek to fix their problem through giving allegiance to false gods in ever-increasing numbers. Jesus sees the more than seven billion people on the planet He created, each having been given the task to worship the Creator, and yet the majority of them are helpless in their spiritually blind condition.

## Hurting

Pain management is a much-needed specialized field in medicine. Every doctor will tell you that when you are wounded, you must stay on top of the pain. If it gets too intense, you'll be overwhelmed. This advice is equally as true for emotional and spiritual pain. We must manage the pain when we hurt.

People go to the greatest lengths to find relief. Some take drugs while others drink to numb the hurt away. Others watch the latest talk show analyst hoping for just one piece of wisdom to help them make it another day. Millions buy the latest self-help books with titles like *10 Easy Steps to Pain-Free Living*. The sad tragedy of all these is when you come to the end of the day, none have permanently relieved your pain. You are stuck on a Ferris wheel of self-soothing that will never fix your problem and the worker at the State Fair who runs the ride has gone to get a corndog. You're trapped!

When Jesus looks at this world He sees people like those just described. They are unable to find relief from the pain of broken relationships, failed marriages, financial failure, problems with children, alcoholism, and drug addiction. You name it and Satan supports it. They are totally stuck in the spin cycle of the washing machine of sin and they wonder if it's even possible for their life to get better.

The good news of the Gospel is the exact prescription God gives to relieve pain of this sort! It is the only ultimate answer for the hurt encountered from the trials of living. And just as Jesus had compassion on those He saw who were harassed and helpless, He was burdened for the hurting too. The good news is that He didn't just hurt for them, He also healed them. Like a good shepherd tending His sheep, Jesus soothed their hurts and provided them relief from the pain of living. If you are hurting right now, please hear these words if you don't get anything else from this chapter. As I've heard Pastor Rick Warren say, "When the tide goes out it always comes back in! God never wastes a hurt!" Be encouraged because God loves you and has compassion for you. He sees the pain and hurt this world has given to you. He is not unaware.

## Hopeless

If you take people who are harassed, helpless and hurting, you can be assured they will encounter hopelessness also. Jesus looks at the world today and sees a growing multitude of hopeless people; people who've tried everything to drown their troubles with no success.

If there is one thing we should be able to spot on the faces of people we meet who are not Jesus followers, it is hopelessness. When we pass them on the streets or go by their desks at work, shouldn't we pray for God to open our eyes to the hopeless plight of people all around? There is nothing worse in life than when the story of your life takes on a dark and sinister look with gray and black as the main colors. We crave the blues, greens, reds, yellows and oranges again but are hopeless and helpless to get them back. Jesus specializes in color restoration and writing new stories for broken lives with bad endings. It is only possible through the Gospel!

When people tell you that their life cannot change, that things will always be bad, do not believe them. Yes, there will always be hopeless, helpless, hurting and harassed people. But God forbid we negate the power of the Gospel of Jesus Christ by agreeing with these that their life cannot improve. If you believe that to be true, you've missed one of the central truths of Christianity. God specializes in bringing good from broken lives full of pain and hurt.

The Gospel is a resolute call to action. It is a call to see the world the way the Lord Jesus sees the world. We cannot harvest fields that we do not recognize to be ripe.

# Fear and Hatred

We can see how Jesus views the world but the question begs to be asked, "How do you view the world?" How does the typical American who sits in a typical evangelical church week after week view the world? Let me give you some thoughts.

## Eyes of Fear

The typical church member views the world through eyes of fear. They have listened to Fox News or CNN far more than they've studied their Bible and have come away with a worldview laden with fear. They witness the atrocities committed by people living seven thousand miles away and fear trumps faith. News agencies specialize in fostering fear and people claiming to be Jesus followers bite like a hungry catfish does at a tasty night crawler.

## Feelings of Hatred

When we hear of Muslim extremists persecuting Jesus followers because of the Gospel, the typical response of many are growing feelings of hatred and anger. Hatred is spawned and fostered by the very ones who must carry forth the Gospel.

I remember sitting one evening in a missionary's home in Bahrain talking with him about his life in a Muslim country. As we talked about how different the Islamic culture is from Christianity, I was impressed with the difficulty of their calling to reach Muslims with the Gospel.

Late in the evening, I remember asking him about an incident I'd heard of a young Muslim woman coming to faith in Jesus and the persecution she faced. Even more, I'd heard that she had been killed by her very own father because she refused to renounce Jesus as Lord. I asked if he would tell me this story so I could tell it to my church. He looked at me and asked me why I would want to go tell a church in America such a story. He then said, "When you do, it will only serve to further the hatred most already feel for Muslims in the Middle East." Message delivered; message received.

I was immediately convicted for playing into the hands of Satan in my desire to relay such a horrible story. It didn't edify, it only fueled a growing incendiary hatred for people no different than us but for location and the truth of the Gospel. Feelings of misplaced superiority rushed over me as I lay in bed that night. Here I was in Bahrain, learning of God's work in this foreign land and I had been more of the problem than the solution.

We in the West should embrace that apart from God's sovereignty, we could just as easily have been born in a Middle Eastern country where the Gospel is not freely preached. Had it not been for the grace of God, we might have lived all our lives wanting the good news of the Gospel, but not having it available to us. But for God's grace we, too, could be shouting cries for Jihad rather than singing "Jesus loves me!" Had you been born in a Muslim country, would you joyfully embrace a Gospel that comes from people you know hate you? I think not!

Let's get this down loud and clear, it is the message God placed in my heart that night...

### You can't harvest those you hate!

Let that truth dive deep into your soul. Jesus says "look out into the fields, they are white unto harvest." He also says that the harvest is plentiful. But let's be truthful, you can't harvest those you hate!

When God looks at the world He does so through eyes of love and He sees rampant *lostness*. He sees a world that is lost; lost people staggering towards hell, people who don't know up from down spiritually. God sees the debauchery of this world and growing *lostness* abounding. He sees our entertainment industries in American and calculates the untold billions spent to desensitize us to the enormity of the *lostness* at hand. He sees entertainers who draw attention through raunchy and immoral acts and He doesn't hate them. He looks at them and knows their situation better than they. They are lost!

The term "lost" is such an unpopular term in religious circles. People don't like the thought that they may be lost. I've never heard a man brag about getting lost in the woods. He'll normally hide that little detail on why he was late getting back to the hunting camp. My wife gets upset with me because I won't stop and ask directions when we're driving unknown roads. I'm not going to admit I'm lost!

No, we don't like the term *lost*. So instead of calling people lost, we embrace our sensitivity training and call them "seekers" or something similar. How dare we be so brash and judgmental to actually say to someone else, "You're lost; you don't know Jesus Christ."

We have been desensitized to the *lostness* around us. It does not even register for most anymore. We are so accustomed to walking past lostness in the grocery store that we are as blind as they and unable to lend them assistance. We sit next to lost people in ballparks on busses and airlines, and we are desensitized to the truth of their situation and silent while all the while we have the answer.

The brutal but biblical truth is that every person, and there are more than seven billion people on planet earth, if they do not put their faith and trust in Jesus Christ alone, they will die and spend an eternity in hell. That's the tragic truth regarding the *lostness* we encounter. They will fall into hell and burn for eternity. They will grasp and grope and seek to find deliverance but it will not come because the Gospel gives no provision for deliverance from hell once there. Why don't we honestly confess to our Lord that we are largely blind to the lostness around us and we make no impact for His Kingdom as a result?

What would happen if we made a firm decision to put aside our fear and hatred and honestly confessed our indifference to God's work in places we'll never travel, to people we'll never meet. How dare we think, "God, those people that live on the other side of the world, if they get saved or if they don't get saved, it's no sweat off my back!" How dare we claim Christ as Savior and have an attitude of indifference such as this?

D. L. Moody, the great evangelist of the middle to late 1800s, was asked one day, "What is the key to your passion for sharing and preaching the Gospel? Why are you so determined to spread the good news?" When asked these questions, Moody and his visitors were up in his office with windows overlooking a crowded street below. Moody told the man to step over to the window and tell him what he saw. The man said, "I see people stirring around down there, that's all. It is just a busy intersection with many people going here and there." "And that is the difference between you and me," Moody said. "When I look down and see those crowds of people, I see lost people. People that if they do not hear the Gospel will go to hell. That is what fuels my passion as an evangelist." What a difference in perspective! One man was jaded and desensitized to the lostness; the other was in tune with it and sought to push it back. One man saw this world with blinded eyes and made little difference; the other saw this world through the compassionate eyes of our Lord and was used to bring monumental change to many for eternity.

Every person reading this book is impacted by the lostness we encounter. Some of you have a lost family member, perhaps a lost spouse. Some have a lost child or a lost grandchild. Some have a lost next door neighbor or a lost person who sits next to you at work every day. *Lostness* is growing all around and we are unwilling to be used by God to repel it and push it back.

Instead we dismiss our responsibility by saying, "Well now we shouldn't judge others. After all, I don't know their heart, only God does." Granted that's true, but when it walks like a duck, quacks like a duck and lays an egg like a duck, we can be pretty sure that it is a duck! If a person is lost, they give evidence of their *lostness*. So why not pray, "God, give me the wisdom and the understanding to be able to determine *lostness* in the world so that I can open my mouth and share the Gospel of Christ with somebody?"

Let's also be very careful to not rewrite the Word of God by our attitudes and actions regarding *lostness*. Satan has numbed so many today to the truth of God's Word that they embrace a new theology that goes like this: "Ok, maybe hell's not really the way it's described in the Bible. Maybe we all do make it to heaven in the end. After all, God's a loving God and wouldn't send anyone to hell." In my church, if I asked all who believe in hell to stand, I feel quite confident that 95% or more would rise to their feet. If I asked them to stand if they believed that the bible they hold in their hands is the inspired and inerrant Word of God, that same 95% would stand. Resoundingly, in conservative evangelical circles we agree that the Bible is the Word of God and that hell is just as real as Heaven. But when we deny our responsibility to share the Gospel with others, we effectively deny the truth of God's Word. We negate what we say we believe when we take the path of convenience rather than the path of obedience and refuse to share the Gospel with others.

Jesus tells us that those who die without having placed their faith in Him as Savior go to hell… end of debate! What we must do is choose obedience over convenience, fear or hatred. Otherwise our actions are speaking louder than our words and it's as if we are saying, "God, I really don't believe Your Word. I really don't believe it's true."

## Embracing Jesus' View of the World

Jesus' view of the world demands action. While some hesitate to embrace this view, if you call Jesus your Lord, you must. On the day you called upon Jesus by faith and received Him as Savior and Lord of your life, on that day you embraced Jesus' view of the world and determined right then that you were supposed to do something with it. A call to do something about the *lostness* we encounter was never intended to be a secondary decision to be made at a convenient time in the future. If I dare call Jesus my Lord, then I am responsible for every command given by Him in the Bible, including going forth into the harvest fields to push back the darkness. So I am not calling you to a level of accountability that you haven't already been called to by Almighty God.

Jesus says in verse 37, "The harvest is plentiful but the laborers (the workers), are few." He looks and sees this magnificent harvest waiting to happen because there are so many ready to be rescued from hell. Jesus sees all the *lostness*, and all that need happen is that the workers go out and work the fields to bring in the great harvest of God. But things haven't changed that much in the last two thousand years. At first, Jesus had thousands of people following Him, enthralled with both His miracles and teaching. Knowing that most were spectators only, Jesus sifted the ranks to arrive at those who were true and obedient followers. After Jesus had risen from the dead and on the day of Pentecost, there was only 120 committed and praying disciples in the Upper Room. Only these were willing to get out of their comfort zone and participate in the harvest.

Jesus says, "The harvest is plentiful but the laborers are few." He never says "the spectators are few." There were many spectators then; there are more today. God is not calling spectators to sit on the sideline and watch others work. He is calling every child of His to respond to His commands to march forward into the harvest fields, carrying the Gospel with them because the crops are ripe.

Years ago, I tried my hand at gardening. I was serving in a small country town and had some wonderful volunteers who were ready to help me plant my corn, potatoes, green beans and tomatoes. To this day I don't know all there is about how to manage a garden, but I did learn this truth: When the crop is ready, pick it! When the corn is ripe, pull the ears. When the green beans are ready, bend over and pluck them from the vine. If the tomato is ripe, gather it up. The produce that was not picked rotted on the vine and was unfit for consumption.

Jesus looks out and sees a ripeness of souls all around and He is calling all Christians everywhere to experience the joy of the harvest. "Harvest is plentiful," He says, "but the workers are few." He wants us to join Him in His work.

If asked to give a mission statement for the Lord Jesus, Luke 19:10 works well. In this verse Jesus says, "For the Son of Man came to seek and to save the lost." His mission centered upon *lostness*. Study Luke chapter 15 and you can see the lost son, the lost sheep, and the lost coin, all illustrating the mission of Jesus to seek and save the lost. It's all about *lostness*. God looks at this world and He sees the *lostness* all around and He knows the only answer for the *lostness* is the Gospel of Jesus Christ.

What is most tragic is that there is a growing contingency in Christianity who will relieve themselves of responsibility by dismissing Jesus as the only way to eternal life. They take a secularist approach to salvation and dismiss God's divine plan with an illogical statement that there "must be multiple paths to God." Please don't fall prey to this trap of Satan. The entire Bible repudiates this and proves this theological error to be false. To settle back in our comfortable chair and cavalierly state that there must be another way to eternal life other than Jesus alone is just a weak attempt to salve a guilty conscience.

There is no other way to eternal life other than Jesus Christ! Jesus said in John 14:6, "I am the way, and the truth, and the life. No one comes to the Father except through me." Our responsibility is to help others know Jesus is the way by being a simple deliverer of the good news of the Gospel. I am nothing more than a messenger boy when I stand to proclaim the Gospel. You are too.

The Word of God is clear in Proverbs chapter twenty-four, verse eleven, "Rescue those who are being taken away to death. Hold back those who are stumbling to slaughter." It is easy to grasp the vivid word imagery used in this verse. People are staggering and stumbling towards a viscous slaughter. Spiritually dead people are stumbling and staggering towards a slaughter where they will spend an eternity falling into an abyss called hell. We might look at that and think, "A loving God wouldn't do that!" and make excuses for ourselves. Let's not make excuses. Let's just embrace the Gospel as the only answer for those stumbling to the slaughter, for those being taken away to death.

At some point, the Apostle Paul realized all of his religious good works were not going to cut it and he was like one stumbling to slaughter, traveling headlong to an eternity in hell. No wonder in Romans he says, "I am unashamed of the Gospel." He made the connection and was unashamed of the Gospel because he was one who had previously been staggering towards the slaughter and was saved. No wonder he's not ashamed! No wonder, in 2 Corinthians 3:12 he tells us that since we have such a great hope in the Gospel message that we should be very bold.

Our calling and our challenge is to honestly embrace Jesus' view of the world if we are ever going to impact this world for Him. Perhaps we need to ask some very important questions at this time, "Lord, what is wrong in my heart when I look at this world as Jesus does and I feel nothing? What is wrong with me inside, God, that I can sit next to somebody who is lost day in and day out at work and never once share the Gospel? What is wrong inside of me that I am ashamed of the Gospel that has given me life through Jesus Christ?"

# Impacting this World

You may be one of the many who feels that you can't do much. You're not blessed with an outgoing personality that allows you to talk easily with people. Or maybe, fear has grasped you by the collar so tight that you can't break free. While I don't believe you have to live in fear, I know that it has incredible power... more than it should in most lives. There is, however, one area where you can join in the work of God immediately and have great impact – prayer! Jesus speaks directly to the compounding need for prayer in verse thirty-eight when He says, "Therefore, pray earnestly to the Lord of the harvest to send out laborers into His harvest."

From a church leader's perspective, I see something taking shape that I've never seen in my years of ministry. I am seeing a laser-like focus on prayer emerge among many in the body of Christ. It's almost as if we've awakened to the reality that we really can't do ministry apart from the power of God found through prayer. We've given it our best shot but have failed miserably. I read a recent statistic on Twitter from Southern Seminary President Albert Mohler regarding our failure in this area. He said, "Between 1994 and 2011, 71.9% of Southern Baptist congregations were either stable or lost members. Only 28% grew." Many factors exist for such dismal statistics; the greatest must surely be prayerlessness.

Among the senior pastors I'm closest to, it's as if we have been slapped and awakened to the dramatic need for prayer. We've sought success through the personality-driven model and most of us have had to admit we don't have that much influence. We've sought church growth through program-driven ministry, but have found that every program regardless of how well promoted fizzles over time. We've sought a new edge through advanced marketing so we can reach a larger percentage of people. This too has paid little dividends over the long haul. There is only one provocative answer and it is prayer!

The music world understands well a phenomenon known as "sympathetic resonance." When multiple pianos are sitting in a room and a chord is struck upon the strings of one piano, the vibrations floating through the air causes the same strings on the other pianos in the room to begin to play a similar but feint sound. The pianos all lift up the same note due to the sympathetic resonance created by the vibrations that began from the original chord being struck.

Where has the sympathetic resonance of prayer gone in the church? We fail to carry forth the Gospel as we should because we do not pray like we ought. Only Jesus guarantees success because the Gospel belongs to Him. Only He can ensure growth and advancement of His Kingdom. When we submit ourselves to Him in prayer, our prayers join with others who pray in similar fashion and we find a sympathetic resonance lifted up to heaven. When this happens, God responds.

## "Thank you for caring!"

Recently I was flying home from Richmond, Virginia. When I got my boarding pass from American Airlines, I knew I was going to be far to the rear of the plane. Little did I know that I would be sitting on the very back row. On this large jet there are two seats on the left side of the aisle and three on the right. The aisle seat on the right side is "D" and that was my seat.

It's uncomfortable because the chair doesn't recline, but that's not the worst part of sitting in "D" seat on the last row. What made this particular seat even more distasteful was that about five feet behind me were two restrooms on each side of the aisle. As this was a 7:15 A.M. flight, everybody had gotten up extra early to make it on time and apparently had consumed extra amounts of their morning java. Once we hit 10,000 feet, the line began forming as people began making their way to the flying Porta-Potty.

Being one of the first on the plane, I was also wondering who was going to be my seatmates. Nobody wants people that are weird to sit by them, especially on the back row. Soon, a husband and wife came down the aisle and took the two seats next to me with the guy sitting in the middle.

I confess that I am not one to talk much on an airplane because I'm usually reading or working. But when packed in like sardines, you almost have to visit with the little "fishy" sitting next to you. We talked for a few minutes while the plane took off and began our trip to Dallas.

When the flight attendant told us it was acceptable to use portable devices, I pulled out my laptop and began writing. For the next 30 minutes the creative juices flowed as I pounded out the words. All the while, the guy next to me kept leaning back to fake a stretch, but I knew he was reading my stuff! Can you believe? Actually I loved it. I was writing a chapter for this book so he was reading the Gospel. I even began praying, "God, I hope he's reading this and that it will speak to his heart as he reads over my shoulder."

After a little while longer, his wife leans across him and asks, "Are you a pastor?" I said, "Yes ma'am, I am." She said, "Oh, that's so good!" We started talking and she told me about the church they'd just begun attending. She then asked me where I pastored and how big my church was. I told her it was pretty good size but I'm not into giving numbers to a stranger so we left it at that. We talked for a few more minutes and then I began writing again.

As we taxied towards the terminal in Dallas, I hear the Holy Spirit inside of me say, "You need to talk to them about Jesus." I am busy, I'm typing and I'm thinking, "God, they've already told me that they go to church, so God I don't need to do that." The Holy Spirit speaks to my heart again, "Byron, it's time that you talk to them about Jesus." I'm typing and responding, "God, I don't really need to talk to them." It's as if God just shouted in my heart, "You're going to preach on *lostness* this coming Sunday, stupid. Don't you think you should talk to them?" I got the message, "Okay, God, I will."

By this time we're at the terminal and people are blocking the aisle all the way to the back on this monster plane. There was no need for the three of us to move. We had 4-5 minutes of sitting before we could deplane. Seizing my opportunity, I leaned in and beckoned they huddle up with me. I said, "I've got to ask you a question. Do you know for certain if you died tonight that you would spend an eternity in heaven?" I sat waiting for a reply. Without a moment of hesitation, she said, "Absolutely we do." I said, "So what you're telling me is both of you are Jesus followers. You've committed your life to Jesus Christ and you're following Him on a daily basis." "Yes, we are," they answered. I said, "Alright. Cool." I'm thinking to myself, "Why did I have to ask them that? God, You knew they were saved, what's the deal?" Here's what happened next. I said, "I certainly hope you're not offended by what I just asked because I wouldn't want to offend you for the world." Before the words were out of my mouth she said, "Oh no, we're not offended. Thank you for caring."

Right then I knew why God wanted me to ask believers in Christ whether they were Jesus followers or not. It was so I could hear four words come forth from her mouth, "Thank you for caring."

God also knew I would include this story for you to read so I could make this closing point. When we care enough to open our mouths and share the Gospel with somebody else, if we do it in the right way their attitude is rarely offense, but often it is "thank you for caring."

The Gospel is worthy of everything – everything – because of what Jesus has done for us. Do we care enough to tell somebody about Jesus Christ? He's the only guaranteed answer to the problem of lostness, pain and suffering in this life.

# chapter 7
## SUFFERING AND THE GOSPEL

I WAS BLESSED THE FIRST TIME I met Walter Kleinard. He was 92 or 93 years old and lived in the local nursing home in the town where I was called to minister. When I walked into the room, his energy as an old man was exhilarating. He would light up the hallways as he buzzed around the nursing home in his wheelchair spreading his joy like a farmer scattering seed. He did all of this while experiencing daily trials and struggles all because of one thing… he'd gotten old. Walter taught many that even in the midst of hardship and suffering, it was possible to smile and spread the Good News to others. I learned much from this man.

I learned the power of perspective. How you view your situation in life makes all the difference. Walter also taught me the importance of a smile. It's not that I was ever against smiling, most people aren't. We just need a reminder of the value of a smile when people are hurting. A genuine smile is an agent of good will in a hard and difficult world. Walter's contagious smile would light up a room. His was powerful!

He also reminded me that regardless of the situation, it is still possible to rejoice. He lived at the nursing home with his wife of 70-plus years. They had a room together, but slept in separate hospital beds against opposite walls. They slept apart and had been married for many decades, yet whenever I'd see Walter, he was usually within very close proximity of his bride. Of course, you always heard Brother Walter quote Scripture. He would begin most conversations with you by quoting Psalm 118, verse 24, "This is the day the Lord has made; let us rejoice and be glad in it." This old gentleman had walked with the Lord for so long that he had it figured out.

I also had reinforced from him the power of married love. As I said, Mr.

and Mrs. Kleinard had been married for around 70 years when one day I was sitting in my office and I received a phone call from the aged groom. My secretary buzzed back and said, "Pastor, Brother Walter is on the telephone." I'm thinking, "Walter Kleinard has never called me before so something must be up. Maybe his wife is sick or something like that."

I jumped on the phone and said, "Brother Walter, what's up?" He said in a loud and emphatic voice, "Brother Byron, I need you to come down here!" I was rather busy at that moment, so I asked, "Why do you need me to come down there, Brother Walter? What's going on?" He said, "I'm upset!" I said, "I can tell by the tone of your voice you're upset. What's gotten you so fired up this morning?" He said, "There's a man around here that keeps messing with my wife and making advances at her and I don't like it one bit so I'm fixing to fight him." I said, "Brother Walter, I'll be right there."

He's 92 years old, in a wheelchair and can't walk by himself. But he's fixing to go 10 rounds with the other guy, who probably can't walk either, for messing with his wife! That is the power of married love, no question about it. Many a younger man could learn something from that to help their marriage today.

As I said, Walter suffered daily and yet he lived his life with a godly perspective, a smile on his face, rejoicing in his heart and, certainly, strength of love for the wife of his youth. But still every day, he suffered. There was probably not a day that passed that he didn't want to be in Heaven. He had long ago embraced the Gospel and had been a devoted Jesus follower for years. And still this gentle man suffered every day while he waited.

The greatest objection to the Gospel for many goes like this: "If God is a good God as you claim, then why does He allow so much suffering and bad to exist in the world? Why do wars and violence exist? Why are innocent people murdered in our cities? Why do diseases like HIV, COPD and Cancer exist? More specifically, why is there even a need for a cancer floor at Texas Children's Hospital in Houston? If God is so good, why would He allow such pain and suffering?" These are legitimate questions deserving legitimate answers. They are not for the faint of heart nor do they merit glib responses from insensitive theologians. These questions stand as a roadblock for many when it comes to understanding the love of God expressed through the Gospel of Jesus Christ.

While there have been untold volumes written on human suffering, in this chapter we will pick at the scab of suffering and see what God's Word has to say. As you have noticed, everything you've read thus far has been related to the power of the Gospel. It should, therefore, come as no surprise to you when I say that the Gospel is the answer for all suffering and pain found in the world today. Our charge is to pay close attention, study God's Word and apply biblical truth correctly. Once done, the questions we have that relate to the perceived injustice of God are answered in the Gospel.

Some of you understand suffering very well; you've walked this painful road much in your life. Most have stood by the casket of someone they love seeking answers that haunt their mind. Perhaps you've personally had a doctor look you in the eye and give a clinical, even sterile diagnosis that you've contracted cancer. Maybe you've been crushed by someone you love who broke your heart. Relational pain is real suffering too. Whatever the reason, we can all speak of times when we've suffered. If not personally, we certainly know others who have suffered because suffering affects every single one of us.

We might affirm the suffering of the wicked as just, but why does a God of tremendous love allow those who are His children to suffer? Why must words like these ever be spoken, "God, if You really love me, then why are you letting me suffer like this? Why am I hurting so much because this feels like anything but love?" These are questions deserving answers.

## The Suffering Apostle

When you study the life of the Apostle Paul, it is crystal clear that this incredibly devoted follower of Jesus suffered greatly. To believe that Christianity exists to remove the threat of physical suffering in this current life runs totally counter to God's Word. Paul carried around in his body a "thorn" in the flesh that brought him continual pain and the God who loves Paul – and who loves us – refused to remove it. Instead, God introduced His servant to the sufficiency of His grace. In 2 Corinthians 12:9 God tells Paul, "My grace is sufficient for you, for my power is made perfect in weakness." With that truth as his balm, Paul trudged onward for the Gospel, carrying his thorn with him.

Paul encountered relentless adversity in his travels. He never walked a road that didn't include a reward of suffering at the destination. This was not a deterrent to Paul's ministry of the Gospel; it was proof of his calling.

In 2 Corinthians 11:24-33, Paul defends his ministry as an apostle of Jesus Christ by pointing to the suffering he experienced. He endured not one but three shipwrecks, being bitten by a poisonous snake, five beatings with the lash, three beatings with the rod, and being stoned. He followed a relentless travel schedule that took him into many dangerous places where his life was often threatened. He faced starvation from lack of food and water and lay half-frozen from cold and exposure. And yet Paul trudged onward for the Gospel, not seeing the suffering as reason to quit but as affirmation that he was doing the Lord's will. Why would Paul put up with so much hardship and suffering? Why would he not quit and find an easy job? What drove him to get up the next day and rejoice in the face of certain danger and suffering? The only acceptable answer is the Gospel!

Paul writes in Philippians 1:12-18: "I want you to know, brothers, that what has happened to me has really served to advance the *Gospel*, so that it has become known throughout the whole imperial guard and to all the rest that my imprisonment is for Christ. And most of the brothers, having become confident in the Lord by my imprisonment, are much more bold to speak the word without fear. Some indeed preach Christ from envy and rivalry, but others from good will. The latter do it out of love, knowing that I am put here for the defense of the *Gospel*. The former proclaim Christ out of rivalry, not sincerely but thinking to afflict me in my imprisonment. What then? *Only that in every way, whether in pretense or in truth, Christ is proclaimed, and in that I rejoice.*" Paul had one purpose for enduring and that was to proclaim the Gospel, and in so doing, he rejoiced.

If we examine Paul's life through worldly eyes, we would never arrive at the idea that Paul had any reason whatsoever to rejoice. He was writing to people he had not seen in four years and during that time had spent two of those years in prison in Caesarea. He is then put on a ship to Rome to appear before Emperor Nero who has no love for Christians. On the way to Rome, he is shipwrecked. When they make it to shore, they begin to build a fire and Paul grabs some brush to build the fire and a venomous snake attaches itself to him. He shakes it off and he goes on while bystanders thought he would die. We know Paul eventually winds up in Rome where he is under twenty-four hour house arrest. Every four hours he gets a new guard. Yet, in spite of all this, the faithful apostle says, "in this I rejoice." What a lesson on perspective in the face of suffering. Quite obviously Paul did not have a theoretical faith; he had a practical faith that he lived in front of others every day. While enduring the most egregious suffering, Paul modeled how to live the Christian life and communicate the Gospel. He revealed several things we can learn to help us understand why suffering is reality for all.

## What is most important in my life?

Suffering filters out the superfluous. Like coffee dripping through a filter to remove unwanted grounds, suffering filters away that which is unwanted and unimportant in the life of every human being. Clearly every person places different values on what they deem to be of worth, but that which they hold most dear will always rise to the surface when pain and hardship enter a life.

Paul's relationship with Jesus was most important to him, and the subsequent communication of the Gospel was priceless. Even a short study of Paul's life reveals that he valued personal relationships, but his call to communicate the Gospel came first.

In verse 12, Paul says, "I want you to know, brothers, that what has happened to me has really served to advance the Gospel." When you read this, the extreme importance Paul placed on the Gospel is obvious. The suffering he faced was not what weighed most heavily on him, it was the fact that in the face of suffering, he saw the Gospel being advanced. In fact, an argument can easily be made that the Gospel was being advanced more while Paul is chained than while he was out preaching daily to others. The Gospel drove this man. The spread of the Gospel was the great goal of this apostle's life. He advanced the Gospel everywhere he went in the face of tremendous pushback and suffering. If there is anyone who could say that he suffered for the Gospel it would be the Apostle Paul.

I have a friend of mine who pastors a church in Hawaii. Quite often, I hear others tell him they would love to come and preach at his church. After all, who wouldn't love an all-expense- paid invitation to minister with Ken for a week. We have been known to accuse Ken of "suffering for the Gospel in Hawaii." Paul's suffering for the Gospel was a far cry from the beautiful sand beaches of Hawaii. Paul is suffering for the Gospel in a Roman prison and what is most important to him has come to the surface.

## Suffering Multiples My Burdens

Suffering results in increased burdens of doctor visits, medical treatments and other unexpected tasks. It draws our attention away from the normality of daily life and causes us to focus on the urgent. Our burden for a solution or cure multiplies exponentially. If a parent is dying of cancer and their child has not become a Jesus follower, the spiritual burden of that mom or dad increases drastically. If one we love begins chemo treatments, the burden of prayer multiples and accumulates. Paul's burden for completing the mission of God in his life and the daily pressure and anxiety for all of the churches he had started continued to grow. Suffering multiplies our burdens.

## Suffering Simplifies My Life

This may sound strange coming on the heels of having just read that suffering multiplies our burdens, but suffering removes much of the clutter, simplifying our lives to what is of utmost importance. When I suffer, my life is scaled down so I can determine what I value most. My greatest treasure is exposed. What we hold most dear is oftentimes found in the middle of the wound of affliction. That which we have taken for granted confronts us with ruthless aggression. Where we have wasted valuable time is seen and corrected. Lists of what we label as extraneous emerge and are culled out of our daily routines. Our lives are simplified when we suffer.

## Suffering Unveils My Deepest Passion

Paul's deepest passion is the Gospel of Jesus Christ. Even in the midst of horrid prison conditions, he's passionate about communicating the Gospel.

Suffering threatens that which we value and hold most dear. It proposes an exchange usually involving time. When what we treasure most is threatened, the lengths we will go to protect it reveal our deepest passion. Like a 9-1-1 call requesting assistance, we respond to the emergency to protect what we are most passionate about. Suffering is often an instrument used by God to unveil our deepest passions.

## Suffering Exposes My Ultimate Priority for Living

There is little doubt that Paul's ultimate priority for living was the Gospel of Jesus Christ. Why else would he willingly endure such tremendous suffering? Paul lived to share the Good News with others. He understood the grim reality that all who die apart from the Gospel suffer an eternity in unquenchable fire. Therefore, regardless of the intensity of his personal suffering, Paul's ultimate priority was the Gospel. He accepted as truth that God was most glorified when His broken and beaten servant stood upon the truth of the Gospel as his ultimate priority.

Why is this not the ultimate priority of every Jesus follower? Why do we not value the Gospel so greatly that we willingly endure suffering in this life in view of the next? Why do we not embrace as our first priority the task of making Jesus famous? Instead we fall prey to petty arguments that mean nothing in God's eternal plan. We argue in our churches over ridiculous matters while many who walk by our buildings would tumble into hell if they dropped dead at that moment. We like to say that the Gospel is a priority to us, but truthfully, we have become calloused and unmoved. We have many priorities, but the Gospel fails to make the list.

Not a day goes by that Christian news sources fail to speak about the on-going persecution of Christians in places like Pakistan, Iran, Yemen, and Somalia. The people in these countries live in daily fear for their lives simply because they have answered God's call to follow Jesus rather than Mohammad. They face constant threat of imprisonment and death all because their priority has become the Gospel. And what does the average Christian in America do? They hop from church-to-church looking for the kind of music from the praise band that best tickles their fancy. They get upset because the preacher goes a little long that morning invading the important plans they had for lunch. They argue in church business meetings on whether to bring in a load of rock to fill the holes in the parking or let people dodge mud puddles on their way into church. They fuss about whether to fix the dishwasher in the parsonage or just let the pastor's wife wash dishes by hand. And then, hypocrisy of hypocrisies, they gather in prayer meetings to request God send revival to their dying church. What they fail to recognize is that the slow death of their congregation is occurring because they have misplaced the most important purpose of the church - carrying forth the Gospel for the glory of God!

God often allows suffering into our life to realign our priorities. He seeks to help me get the treasure, passion and priority in my life where it need be so that I can understand and begin to do the things that honor Him most. You might ask, "Why does God have to do that? Why must He go to the extremes of suffering to get our attention?" Let me explain it like this. There is a lot of what I'll call "junk" in this world that the devil and his accomplices throw our way to put a damper on our spirituality. Wouldn't you agree? That junk serves to smother out the work of God in our life. While God desires to do a great work in every life, the junk of this world quickly smothers the work of God so that we lose all effectiveness for Him. And sadly, we are often drawn more to the junk this world offers than a deep, personal relationship with Jesus. We are smothered by the unimportant.

When I was a boy growing up in Southeast Texas, we lived on two heavily wooded acres. Every year the leaves would fall and one of my jobs was raking the leaves. Because we lived in the country, we didn't bag the leaves for the trash collector, we burned them. I realize for some, this is hard to grasp and seen as pollution. Perhaps it was, but at that time, it was the neighborhood norm and nobody cared.

I would rake the leaves into large piles and then carry each pile individually to be burned. Everything was good until I brought the next large load of leaves and threw them on the pile. Quite often they were damp on the bottom and would smother the fire so that all you had was thick yellow smoke, but no fire.

Because of all the junk we face in the world a lot of Christians have some smoke rising but there's no fire. There's no visible blaze of the working of God in their life. Their passion for the Gospel is gone. Our ultimate priority is the junk smothering out God's work. There's a lot of smoke but there's not a lot of fire.

Sometimes God brings suffering our way so that a passion for what He deems most important can be ignited into flame. We don't like to think of this as a possible reason for pain and hardship, but it aligns with God's Word. The fact that God would bring suffering to us for the purpose of helping us define our ultimate priority is thoroughly biblical, even loving. Let's not quickly dismiss Hebrews 12:6 that tells us "the Lord disciplines the one He loves and chastises every son whom He receives." After all, He is the perfect Father.

God did this with the nation of Israel and He does it with individuals today. In Hosea 12:6 God says, "When I fed them they were satisfied. When they were satisfied, they became proud. Then, they forgot me." Did you catch that? It was only after they were satisfied with the good things from God's hand that they developed spiritual amnesia. Their satisfaction with God's provision was greater than their satisfaction with God. They became proud when their bellies and pockets bulged, so proud that they forgot God.

Do you find your satisfaction more with the "things" this life offers or do you find your satisfaction in God? Are you more satisfied by the "junk" that serves to smother your passion for God or has pride enveloped your heart and you have forgotten Him? I understand that theoretically most deny that they've forgotten God, but what about practically? Does your life exhibit a flaming Christianity regardless of the trials you face or are you just a smoldering pile that does little more than pollute the cause of Christ? Whether we like it or not, suffering often serves to define what is most important in our lives, drawing us to God.

## Do I have the proper perspective?

Paul had an incredible perspective for living. Walter Kleinard had a proper perspective on life. When I saw him, his godly perspective rubbed off on me because he was always encouraging, always looking to the future with expectancy. Perspective is important. In the face of suffering, sometimes it's everything. How our perspective is focused makes all the difference.

Many years ago, a young Jewish shepherd came running into his tent full of excitement. His wife looked at her out of breath husband and asked him why he was so worked up. He said, "Oh my love, remember the old ewe we thought was barren? She gave birth to twins lambs today and I'm so excited about it. You know what I think we should do? I think we should give one of those new lambs to the Lord." She smiled at her husband and agreed. The next day her husband came into the tent at midday and was just as down as he was up the day before. She said, "Joshua, what is wrong with you, yesterday you were so happy and today you are so sad?" He looked at his wife and said, "Abigail, do you remember the two lambs that I told you about yesterday?" She nodded her head. He said, "Well the one dedicated to the Lord just died!"

While we laugh at this story, we know that the perspective we sometimes have regarding the things of God is not too different than that Jewish shepherd. The junk I described a moment ago clouds our perspective so that we do not see things as we should.

But when reading verse 12 again, Paul gives no evidence he is confused or clouded in his perspective. None! He says, "I want you to know, brothers, that what has happened to me has really served to advance the Gospel." In other words, all these chains, the guards, and everything else, have not stood in the way of the Gospel but has propelled it forward. I can easily imagine Paul smiling with joy in his heart as he writes these words on the parchment. Maybe his memory took him back to the trials of Joseph the next to last son of Jacob in the Old Testament book of Genesis. In chapter fifty and verse twenty the New International Version reads, "You intended to harm me, but God intended it for good to accomplish what is now being done, the saving of many lives." That's a godly perspective for sure!

The proper perspective in Paul's life helped him to advance the truth so that all of the suffering Satan threw his way to smother the Gospel did just the opposite, serving as fuel to propel it forward instead. Just as Joseph could look back and see God at work even while he was sold into slavery and falsely accused, Paul could see God at work every time something tragic came his way. How could Paul live with such a divine perspective? Here's the answer...

*Paul was focused on the furtherance of the Gospel;*
*Paul was not focused on the furtherance of Paul.*

Does that make sense? The great apostle cared far more about the Gospel than he did himself. He cared more about the advancement of the Gospel and so he believed that regardless of his trials, the Gospel could and would move powerfully into Rome. The entire tone of Paul's letter to the Christians in Philippi is from a positive perspective. He does not see his suffering as punishment for having persecuted the church. He does not see his suffering as punishment for having been a "meanie" to Christians or anything like that. He sees his suffering as the will of God in his life. Paul had the unique ability to see everything and every situation through the eyes of God. That is perspective. That is Christian perspective. And because we live in a fallen world where suffering impacts every person, we must learn to look beyond the moment and see the hand of God. He is writing a far greater and much grander story if we can just recognize His hand upon the pen.

## My Personal Story

When I was a 6-year-old little boy I got up one morning and headed down the stairs of our house in St. Louis, Missouri. When I rounded the corner and entered the living room, my mother was seated in one chair, the next door neighbor in another and my 8-year-old brother, Mark, on the floor. I knew something was wrong because my mother was crying. When I climbed into her lap she told me that my daddy had died that night. This was the furthest thing from my childlike mind so I looked at her and with a laugh said, "No, he didn't." Everything changed seconds later when I realized momma wasn't joking as she explained he'd died of a massive heart attack. Even after so many years I can tell of every event that transpired over the next few days with clarity.

We immediately left St. Louis and flew to Texas on our journey home. The airline we flew struggled to load daddy's casket and was delayed in taking off. The captain came back and spoke with my mother personally about the need to leave my father's body behind to be brought on a later flight. While I didn't understand what this young widow was feeling, I gained a great sense of her loss as she stood before his casket begging her 34-year-old husband to wake up. He did not, the reality of death ensured that would not happen... yet.

We soon settled into a new normal in the little country town where we lived. I was in the second grade when school began after that painful summer. While we were all so very lonesome, we managed to move forward in our grief. We attended church weekly, spent time with family and friends, rode our horses and allowed time to pass. And pass it did. The years moved on for the three of us, bringing happiness and joy with them.

As we began the school year of 1977, Mark was a senior and I was a sophomore in high school. Mother was seeing a man who would eventually become her husband. Life was good as we looked expectantly into the future.

Football, playing trombone in the band, pep rallies, and worrying about who to ask to the homecoming dance were high priorities for me until September 24, 1977.

In the early hours of the morning, I was awakened to my mother screaming. I jumped out of bed and ran to our living area to a repeat of what I had experienced in 1969, only this time my brother wasn't in the room. There my mother sat on the floor. Two ladies from our neighborhood were also there along with the pastor from our church. As I looked at my pastor, he grabbed me by both arms and said, "Byron, Mark died tonight." It was as simple as that. My brother had been rabbit hunting with a friend, something he'd done regularly for quite some time. On this particular night his truck wouldn't crank. So he jogged to the barn to get the tractor and a chain to pull the truck back to the barn. When he rounded a curve in the road, perhaps going too fast, the tractor went into the ditch and flipped on my brother, killing him instantly.

To say that my life was turned upside down doesn't do justice to what I felt. I was raw with waves of grief flooding over my naked emotions. In my mind I could not come to terms with why God had allowed additional suffering of this magnitude in my life. I did not feel then, nor do I today, that God brought about the pain in my life just to see my reaction. That is not how a loving God treats His children. I do believe everything that has come my way has been filtered through His hands like sand through an hour glass. I realize that He saw what was transpiring that night and could have stopped it before Mark went down the hill and into the ditch. In His sovereignty, God elected to not do so. Instead, in the years ahead God sought to purposefully change my perspective so that I could see my life verse, Genesis 50:20, take shape and develop. He replaced my flawed perspective with His divine one and brought healing to my brokenness. He did that for me and, just as easily, He can do the same for you. As I shared in a previous chapter, Pastor Rick Warren is right, "God never wastes a hurt. When the tide goes out it always comes back in." He specializes in taking our broken perspective and transforming it into triumph. He knows how to redirect our faulty emotions so that we can see His hand of goodness holding the pen that rights our story. God is good!

## Daily Perspective

The longer I live, the more convinced I become that God helps us manage difficult circumstances by reminding us that life is 90% attitude or perspective and 10% of the other stuff. Have you found that to be true in your life? What a difference it makes when we see God at work especially in the middle of our pain. When we have a smile on our face and others know the trials we face, in a similar manner as Paul's situation, doesn't what has happened to us really serve to advance the Gospel? I think it does.

Why do so many Christians battle daily with runaway emotions? Many seem to struggle as much if not more than hopeless non-Christians. As a Jesus follower, are we not supposed to view life differently? Why do we not live with this overwhelming abundance of joy that is ours for the taking every single day? Can't we agree that every day should be a little like Christmas for the believer in Jesus Christ? Every day shouldn't we embrace the truth that our God is good and He gives good gifts? Out of His great love and mercy, He has saved us by His grace. That fact alone should transform our faulty perspective into one of hope enabling us to rejoice that today is going to be a good day!

Having a proper perspective every day helps us stand against the multitude of "Joy Killers" in the world. Too many Jesus followers allow other people and circumstances to push their buttons and steal their joy. Someone doesn't respond as we think on social media and we are crushed under the weight of perceived rejection. We get our feelings hurt at work when someone looks at us a little funny and we find ourselves muttering, "Just who does he think he is, acting all high and mighty?" You know what I mean; we've all been guilty of muttering under our breath before. When we handle our daily life situations with such a poor perspective, it is little wonder why we do not have the joy and happiness God intends. Besides, if Paul can be overflowing with joy from a prison cell – that's right, a Roman prison cell where mercy and grace are nonexistent – then you will never convince me that you can't be overflowing with joy from the luxury of your four or five bedroom home. My prayer is that God would help us be more like Walter Kleinard and say, "This is the day that the Lord has made. I will rejoice and be glad in it!" And if you were Walter Kleinard, you'd be shuffling along with your feet pushing your wheelchair, but you'd have overflowing joy inside because of the simple Gospel of Jesus Christ!

My son was home from college recently when over lunch he shared his thoughts about the importance of attitude and perspective in life. He asked me, "Dad, remember the movie, *Monsters University*? When Sully and Mike couldn't make it on the scare floor, they found themselves working in the mail room, remember that?" I nodded because I knew he was onto something. He said, "Sully and Mike started in the mail room and had such tremendous attitudes that they began their career by putting up little signs stating their goal to be the best mail room employees they could possibly be. That's the kind of attitude and perspective you need to get ahead in life. If you're going to work in the mail room, be the best mail clerk ever and see what happens next!" What an awesome word from someone who gets it! Many adults far older than my son haven't figured out the value of a good attitude. Checking your attitude before you leave for work every morning should be as routine as setting your home security alarm. If we'd just get our attitude right and embrace God's perspective for the day, we wouldn't suffer needlessly because of failure to do so from the start.

## Do I understand my purpose for living?

If there is anybody who understood his purpose for living, it was Paul the apostle. He was under no preconceived idea that he would ever do anything else other than be a missionary church planter. Now in prison, he still knows that in the timing of God he will still present the Gospel in Rome, after that only God knows his future. Paul understood his purpose so very, very well. In verse 13 the Apostle says, "So that it has become known throughout the whole imperial guard and to all the rest that my imprisonment is for Christ."

Notice the last phrase, "my imprisonment is for Christ." That's Paul's purpose! He's imprisoned for the Gospel just as he is a prisoner of the Gospel of Jesus Christ. He's bound by the Gospel. He can't do anything to change his circumstances. He calls none of the shots in his life. He doesn't direct his path. He has no voice of his own. He was simply to be a spokesman for God, saying what God would have him to say as His prisoner of the Gospel of Jesus Christ. Paul was sold out and committed as a prisoner who would suffer for the Gospel.

When God called Andi and me into the ministry, only then did we really understand how tough this calling would be. I dare not minimize the struggles you face because life is hard regardless of vocation. But when we entered full-time ministry and began to experience hardship, we were shocked by what some less spiritually-minded individuals would say. We heard statements like this, "If it were really God's will that you be in the ministry, why are you suffering so much? Why is it so difficult and hard?" When something this ridiculous was said, I would find myself wanting to ask, "Have you even read the Bible? Because it's obvious you know zero about theology and shouldn't be giving spiritual advice to anyone."

If Paul is any indication, and I sure think he is, then I stand convinced that the suffering someone incurs due to the Gospel can often be seen as absolute proof of being deep inside the will of God. When you're dead center in God's will, suffering happens; you have hard and difficult times. Things rarely seem to go the way you want. The Apostle Paul was directly in the will of God and yet, he experienced horrendous pain, hardship, difficulty and suffering. It was God's will and purpose for Paul that he suffer for the Gospel. When he encountered the risen Lord Jesus on the road to Damascus, the fact of his coming suffering was explicitly made known. Jesus says in Acts 9:16 of Paul, "I will show him how much he must suffer for the sake of My name." So even in prison, Paul was living out his purpose.

Many have found the strength they needed to persevere during hard times through a careful study of the leading men and women whom God uses mightily. Adoniram Judson was one such person. He was the first foreign missionary sent from America to distant shores.

Judson arrived in Burma in 1813 to begin the arduous process of spreading the Gospel to people who had never heard the name of Jesus. Nobody was waiting to welcome his arrival. He was not wanted. When he began preaching the Gospel, he was shunned. Over time, however, Judson took upon the task of translating the Burmese language so that he could assemble a little Burmese grammar in hopes of better communicating the Gospel. He labored 14 years before completing the first Burmese grammar booklet. During that period of time, Adoniram Judson had buried one wife and multiple children in the family cemetery. He was there almost forty years and sometimes it seemed that the Judson family cemetery grew more in Burma than the Gospel spread. Later on, he said these words regarding his years of painful suffering, "If I had not felt certain that every trial was ordered by infinite love and mercy, I could not have survived my accumulated sufferings." I get that. If you are experiencing the magnitude of loss of those family members most precious to you, it is only the love of God coupled with a divine purpose that can move you to persevere.

In his personal diary, Judson tells of the pain he experienced when his second wife, Sarah, died and he subsequently boarded a ship with his children to return to America:

> For a few days, in the solitude of my cabin, with my poor children crying around me, I could not help abandoning myself to heart-breaking sorrow. But the promise of the Gospel came to my aid, and faith stretched her view to the bright world of eternal life, and anticipated a happy meeting with those beloved beings whose bodies are mouldering at Amherst and St. Helena. It was a long, sad voyage home.[5]

The hope of the Gospel is what carried Judson through his darkest hours of grief. It is the same hope we have today that regardless of the pain and hurt, God has a plan and a purpose that is always good.

If you remember a few pages earlier when I described the personal losses I'd encountered with the death of my father and brother, I stated that death ensured my father would not arise from the grave... yet. Remember that? Let me explain what I mean. Just as Judson had a strong confidence he would again see his loved ones whom he'd buried in Burma, I have equal confidence that my relatives will also rise and I will see them again. Scripture leaves no doubt that God has planned a great reunion for those who follow Jesus.

Every believer in Christ will one day slip free from the bonds of this fallen world and enter eternity. Once there we will worship the Lord Jesus forever. We will be so enraptured by His presence that for a million years we won't shift our focus from the glorious King on His throne. Time will have fled and we will be consumed with the splendid inheritance we receive in His honor. At that time, I will be with my Christian loved ones again. While

---

5    Courtney Anderson, *To the Golden Shore: The Life of Adoniram Judson* (Valley Forge: Judson Press, 1987), 441.

I am waiting for decades to see them now, they are not anxiously waiting for time to drift slowly by so they may see me. They are consumed with splendor untold as their full enjoyment of Heaven has begun. The Gospel ensures that this reunion will take place. This is not simply wishful dreaming by lonesome pilgrims on earth. It is biblical truth that cannot be dismissed. We will be reunited with our loved ones who've gone to Heaven first. We will experience a great reunion in the clouds with the Lord Jesus being the central focus. We will spend eternity doing as God wills in Heaven together. We will see our Christian loved ones, know them, love them, hear them, and talk with them. We will celebrate Christ's glory around the throne together forever! Adoniram Judson was exactly right! The promise of the Gospel does come to our aid during the darkest hours on earth as we grasp all that it promises. There is always a divine purpose to the suffering we experience.

# Life's Most Passionate Sermon

Paul was a passionate man with a deep love for God and doing His will. We've discussed his passion for the Gospel. I'm also convinced from Scripture that Paul had a passion for preaching God's Word. When he preached, he employed persuasive powers carried along by the Holy Spirit. There are multiple references in scripture to Paul preaching and sharing the Good News. Some of which give us preachers great encouragement.

On one particular evening, Paul was preaching long into the night while a young man named Eutychus sat in a window listening. The fire from the lamps had warmed the room and the Middle Eastern night air had grown still. Paul had preached for a long while, long enough to begin losing the attention of some in the room. Suddenly, Eutychus drifted off to sleep and fell out the window to the street three stories below... dead! There is not a preacher alive who can't draw some encouragement from the fact that even when Paul preached some slept.[6]

There is something special about preaching and communicating the Word of God. Whether it's two or three people, 300 or 3,000, it doesn't matter, it's special. We all agree, however, that most will never stand to

---

6    To read the entire story of Paul miraculously raising Eutychus from the dead, see Act 20:7-12.

preach a sermon behind a pulpit. But let's never doubt that every person reading this book is preaching a sermon with their life.

When you read the passage from Philippians again, you recognize at that time in the apostle's ministry, Paul was preaching more with his life than with his mouth from that Roman prison. Imagine that, God's great apostle was preaching so loudly from his suffering that he was inspiring many others to preach the Word boldly. The Bible says in Philippians 1:14, "And most of the brothers, having become confidant in the Lord by my imprisonment are much more bold to speak the word without fear." This is the result of watching and hearing reports of Paul's precarious position. He is in prison and they are watching his life and Paul said, "Because of my imprisonment others [the brothers in Christ] are much more bold to speak the word about Jesus Christ." Paul had been a preacher with his mouth for years. Now Paul was preaching his most passionate sermon through the suffering he was experiencing due to the Gospel he so dearly loved.

Every Jesus follower is a preacher! You may not wish for the title, but you are a preacher nonetheless. You may even rebel at the thought of me designating every disciple of Christ a preacher. My answer would be that because you claim Christ as your Savior, people are watching you. By the life they live, some people preach magnificent sermons that linger in the minds of others for years. Walter Kleinard would be an example of someone who preached an excellent sermon with his life.

Some preach "so-so" sermons. Some days they are spot on in their walk with God and some days they are anything but. Some preach sermons that fall flat, causing others to reject their message by saying, "What they have is not anything I want." Some preach boring sermons about Jesus Christ. Can you imagine that, being boring about Jesus? Some people preach sermons that are full of hypocrisy because they claim Jesus on Sunday and on the other six days of the week they preach with their life that Jesus doesn't matter to them at all. We've all met those people.

Every person who embraces a call to follow Jesus for salvation is preaching a sermon and the most passionate sermon they will ever preach is when they suffer. Whenever a Christian goes through times of pain and suffering, people watch what they will do next. They want to know how the Jesus follower they work with or the one they live down the street from will handle the pain of adversity once it has accosted them. Curious people are always watching those in pain to see how they respond. You should never doubt that the most passionate sermon you will ever preach is when you are facing your greatest trials and you don't even need to open your mouth. Saint Francis of Assisi once said, "Preach the Gospel at all times. If necessary, use words."

I am reminded of Bill Bright, the founder of Campus Crusade for Christ. He was a faithful follower of Jesus for many years, being used by God to lead many thousands of college students to faith in Christ. Late in life, Bill contracted lung cancer and found himself preaching his most passionate sermon amid an array of tubes, needles, chemotherapy and oxygen. In his book, *The Journey Home – Finishing with Joy,* he details his singular fear during those last days when he struggled for every breath. His great fear was not death. Bill Bright knew that death would be his release to live in the presence of God. He was not afraid to die. Instead, Bill was afraid that in the midst of overwhelming pain that he might dishonor God by something he would say or through his actions. He was afraid that his final sermon would not be preached well. He said, "I want to be faithful to my last breath, praising Him and rejoicing as I go." How can we not admire that type resolve when witnessing someone suffering so greatly while preaching so passionately?[7]

My prayer for every reader is that when this book is closed and we walk forward in life, that we do so with the same resolve and determination of Bill Bright. My prayer is that you will give all your effort in preaching your life sermon with passion and power for the glory of God. The most effective life sermon must begin with a consuming passion for God. Without which the sermon you preach can never bring God the glory He deserves.

It is followed by a passion for God's Word. No preacher can preach with boldness without spending time in God's Word.

There must also be a passion for God's will. If I choose to live outside of God's will, my preaching will fall flat and be detrimental to the Kingdom of God.

Finally, to preach powerfully with my life, I need a passion for God's Gospel because the Gospel is good news, not bad. It's good news yearning to be shared with others.

---

7    Bill Bright, *The Journey Home – Finishing with Joy* (Nashville, TN: Thomas Nelson Publishers, 2003), 11.

I have witnessed many people nullify their ability to preach with their mouth because of a life lived in disobedience to God. They lose credibility as a Christian and become unwilling to open their mouth and proclaim the Gospel because their life is in such a horrible mess that it refutes everything they say. What would happen if you chose from this day forward to preach your most passionate sermon by the way you live? What would happen? You don't even need to open your mouth, just live in such a way that it's as if you are saying to others, "Examine me to see if you can find Jesus in my life, not only in my words." What would happen? Why not find out?

# Maximum Glory

Do you want to know what suffering in the Christian life is really all about? We've followed Paul's description of God's working through his sufferings and we arrive at the ultimate purpose for Christian suffering. Paul concludes this passage with the resolute statement that regardless of the pain and the hardship that he faces, it's all been for the proclamation of the Gospel of Jesus Christ, and he has chosen to rejoice. Look at verse 18 where Paul says, "What then? Only that in every way, whether in pretense or in truth, Christ is proclaimed, and in that I rejoice."

Paul cared about one thing exclusively – that Christ be proclaimed. It didn't matter his circumstances. What other people said about him was deemed unimportant by Paul. All that mattered to Paul was that Jesus Christ was proclaimed through the only life he had to live. By this point in his pilgrimage, Paul was so comfortable in his trust of God that whatever came his way he would rejoice. He had grown quite familiar in his service through suffering and he knew that the greatest glory he could ever give to Almighty God was found in submission to the hardship he faced. Paul would endure; he would persevere with rejoicing! Regardless of the hurts that tracked with him through life, regardless of the thorn he carried or the scars on his body, regardless of the abandonment he felt from others, as long as Christ was proclaimed Paul rejoiced. Until the day he would die, Paul would glory in the Gospel of the Lord Jesus Christ and seek to advance the Gospel regardless of what came his way.

Galatians 6:14 tells us Paul's attitude, "But far be it from me to boast except in the cross of our Lord Jesus Christ, by which the world has been crucified to me, and I to the world." As such, the pain, beatings, the number of times he would be stoned, or the cruelty of a Roman jailer didn't matter. Paul did what he did for the glory of Christ. He was surrendered in his service to the Gospel of Jesus Christ for the glory of God. That's what it's all about! Paul had figured it out. He lived every day to maximize the glory of God with his life.

Could this good God whom we love have taken all of Paul's pain away in an instant? Of course He could. Could He remove all of the pain and suffering we feel, all of the heartache in this life for every Jesus follower? Of course He could! Could He remove the pain of death? Of course! The answer to all of these questions is "Yes!" Then why doesn't He? Why does this God who loves us so much that He sent His only Son to die for us, why does He allow so much suffering among His children? Here's the final answer.

If God snapped His finger and said, "No more suffering, pain, hardship or anything of the sort," Satan would cry foul! He would immediately scream, "You cheated!" and would then claim victory over God for having removed the instrument of pain. Satan's belief is that the only reason you are a Jesus follower and reading this book is because God has blessed you. He denounces your love for God as real, choosing to believe that you don't love Him, you only love His benefits. Satan would say to God, "They would not love You for who You are, nor would they worship You as Sovereign Lord, if You took away all their pain and suffering. They would love the benefits of living in a painless, suffering-free world, but they could never say that they loved You more than the benefits received from Your hands. But you keep them pinned down with pain and suffering, they won't love You then either. In fact, they will deny You and refuse to worship You if You increased their suffering." Either way, Satan would ruthlessly proclaim himself victorious.

Do you remember the book of Job in the Old Testament? In the opening chapters, Satan stood in the presence of God, accusing Job of worshiping God only because of God's protection on his life. But take away the blessings of family and good health and Satan was convinced Job would curse God and deny His goodness. Job did nothing of the sort. He refused to sin against God even in the midst of the rawest form of suffering.

This brings me to my conclusion and the ultimate reason for the pain we encounter. The greatest answer to the problem of suffering is seen when as human beings we receive the Gospel by faith with no promise of pain-free living on this side of eternity. When by faith alone, you call upon God and proclaim, "Lord, I don't understand why I'm hurting and in this incredible pain. But Lord, I trust you regardless of the pain and suffering that comes my way. By faith I believe in Jesus as the only Son of the living God for salvation." When this occurs, God is glorified to an infinite level by His creation.

Nothing proves my love for God like obedience to Him in the face of incredible hardship. When you suffer, and yet remain unmoved in your faith, God is glorified exponentially. His greatest glory comes from those who receive the gift of salvation and then faithfully walk with Him regardless of pain and suffering. When this is done, continual praise and glory to God is lifted high as Habakkuk 2:14 is carried forth as our testimony. Our life shouts, "For the earth will be filled with the knowledge of the glory of the Lord as the waters cover the sea."

Suffering will continue to exist until the end of time so that Satan will have no validity in his claim of a moral victory. Besides, should you awaken one morning and all pain, suffering, heartache, struggle, and conflict is gone, you will have awakened in Heaven and that will be alright too. But in the interim, let's trust God. Let's believe that God has a plan and purpose for all of the hurt that we encounter. Let's preach boldly with our lives as we walk through the valley of the shadow. And let's not forget that the world watches always to see how Jesus followers react when suffering falls upon them. So preach loud and bold for the Gospel of Jesus Christ. Live loud for Jesus so that you're preaching a good sermon to those around you every day. Bring honor and glory to God regardless of the circumstances of this life.

On April 25, 2004, I stood behind a pulpit and before me was a casket. Brother Walter Kleinard, who was ninety-five years of age, had gone to see the Lord he loved just a couple of days before. As I stood there and preached that man's funeral service, it was a time of incredible joy. My text that day was: "This is the day the Lord has made, let us rejoice and be glad in it." When I finished the funeral I sat behind my desk and wrote these words in my journal about Walter, "Ninety-five year old sweet saint of God who loved Jesus till the end." What a story!

# chapter 8
## HOLES IN THE KNEES OF OUR PANTS

THE YEAR 1849 SAW HORDES of people migrating to the West in search of gold. On one particular California day, one of the gold miners walked into a textile shop with a problem and said to the man working there, "I need your help!" The guy looked at him and asked how he might be of assistance. "Look at my trousers," the miner said, pointing to the holes in both knees of his pants. He went on to say, "We miners do most of our work on our knees. The problem is we wear the knees of our pants out in six months or less. They should last longer than that." The man looked at his knees, assessed the situation and said, "You know, you're exactly right. We probably should use a different material. We've got some material that's canvas that we actually make tents out of. Why don't you let me make you a pair of trousers out of that material and let's see how that works?" So the shop keeper proceeds to make a pair of trousers out of the strong canvas material. It was not long after that fateful day that most men in the mining fields of California could be found wearing Levi Strauss trousers because of their strength and resiliency. They held up under the daily grind of working on their knees.

For the Jesus follower, we don't mine gold, but we are most definitely called to work on our knees! Prayer is the hardest possible work we can do, and it is most often done on our knees. It's where the follower of Christ kneels before God, crying out and requesting He move mightily. Urgent prayer is calling out to God, asking Him to respond with great expectation.

I have spent a number of chapters describing this incomparable gift of the simple Gospel of Jesus Christ. I think by this point you have been able to surmise that the Gospel excites me tremendously. I know that the

Gospel is the answer to every problem and issue we face in life. I live with an overwhelming burden that people whose lives are flat lined and in a state of emergency will find the answers they need through the Gospel.

We often wonder why we feel so little of God's presence in our life, the answer is not a deficiency in the Gospel, it is our deficiency when it comes to prayer! David Jeremiah, pastor of Shadow Mountain Community Church in El Cajon, California describes the crisis of prayerlessness like this, "One of the reasons we are so worn out from life is because our knees aren't."[8]

In this chapter, I confess that it is my goal to issue a strong challenge. If I can challenge you to take what you read on these pages as encouragement to spend more time on your knees in prayer, I will have been successful. So pause for moment and do a personal assessment. How much time do you spend in prayer on a daily basis? How often do you pray, daily, weekly, monthly or only in an emergency situation? Would you classify your prayer life as bold and powerful or timid and anemic? Do you feel you are praying enough and that God is pleased with the amount of time you spend communicating with Him? Answer these questions. Be truthful. We gain nothing unless we are willing to have our faults laid bare.

## Possibilities Galore

Once a person embraces the simple Gospel of Jesus Christ to become a Jesus follower, at that precise moment an entire array of beautiful possibilities opens. The myriad of promises found in the Bible become theirs. The journey of a lifetime is embarked upon. The joy of knowing that we have a Savior who is right by our side through thick or thin is discovered. All of this is only because of the simple Gospel of Jesus Christ. The Gospel makes all things new and more focused for the follower of Jesus. It introduces him to the delightful saving grace of God and then opens up an unlimited amount of power and potential found through prayer.

The Gospel alone provides and ensures the validity of our prayers. The common belief that God hears all prayers, even the prayers of those living in rejection and rebellion of His Son, is a myth. The Gospel is the avenue that makes true prayer possible. It alone opens the channel between God and

---

8    David Jeremiah, *Signs of Life* (Nashville, TN: Thomas Nelson, 2007), 83.

His creation. For the first time in our life we find that we are tuned into the broadcast channel of God.

When I was a boy growing up in the country, we didn't have cable television and the thought of gaining a broadcast signal from a satellite was sci-fi all the way. Our television received a signal from the only three major networks in existence: ABC, NBC and CBS. The problem was that our exterior antenna would sometimes need adjustment so we could see a clear picture. On many nights as we sat watching TV, my mom would ask me to go outside, to the side of our house, and turn the antenna so that we would get a little more clarity on our set. Most nights that did the trick.

When I confessed Jesus Christ as my Savior and received the glorious gift of eternal life, my spiritual antenna was tuned into God's channel for the very first time in my life. I was no longer living in the gray world of fuzzy spiritual thoughts that might have given me a warm feeling but lacked true substance. Instead, my spiritual antenna was turned so that I could now receive God's signal in high definition.

I share this because we all need to understand that the Gospel opens up a life of high definition living in relationship to God for all who will confess Jesus. God hears our prayers because we have placed our faith in His Son.

For years it has been debated and discussed whether God hears all prayer. Conservative Christians have stood against the grain of worldly logic and profoundly stated that apart from Jesus, the Creator does not hear the prayers of the billions who walk this earth in lostness. When challenged, a number of answers from the Bible can be used to support this conclusion, but the primary one is really very simple. The Jesus follower prays to the one true and living God. We do not believe in a plethora of all-powerful, all-knowing, all-present gods. We believe there is only one true God who hears and responds to our prayers. Because the words of Peter's confession found in Matthew 16:15 have become our own, the prayers we pray are quite different. We affirm fully the powerful confession of the Apostle Peter, "You are the Christ, the Son of the living God."

## Jesus and Prayer

In Matthew chapter 7, the Lord Jesus is closing out the greatest sermon ever preached, the Sermon on the Mount. In so doing, He begins to talk again about prayer. He had begun the sermon with prayer, sharing a model through which we can learn how to pray. You've probably read or quoted that prayer yourself. It goes like this...

Our Father in Heaven, hallowed be Your name.
Your Kingdom come, Your will be done, on earth as it is in Heaven.
Give us this day our daily bread, and forgive us our
debts, as we also have forgiven our debtors.
And lead us not into temptation, but deliver us from evil.
For yours is the kingdom and the power and the glory, forever. Amen
Matthew 6:9-13

In this wonderful sermon, Jesus now feels it important to begin His conclusion by once again focusing the crowd on the necessity of prayer. Matthew 7:7-11 says, "Ask, and it will be given to you; seek, and you will find; knock and it will be opened to you. For everyone who asks receives, and the one who seeks finds, and to the one who knocks it will be opened. Or which one of you, if his son asks him for bread, will give him a stone? Or if he asks for a fish, will give him a serpent? If you then, who are evil, know how to give good gifts to your children, how much more will your Father who is in heaven give good things to those who ask him!"

These verses are filled with promise for every believer. Jesus is telling us that if we will just ask, if we will get down on our knees and begin to ask God, that God will move in a mighty way. He points us to the absolute necessity of calling out to God in prayer to see Him moved to action.

The reason we do not have spiritual awakening in America today is because the church of the Lord Jesus Christ is not getting on their knees and asking God to sweep across this nation. If we began to pray as Jesus instructs, crying out to God in great fervency, we would see God move mightily. He would begin to restore many things we hold dear. We would see God bring healing to our land and do greater works than we could ever comprehend because none of us have lived through a true spiritual awakening. We've read of them in history books, but we have never lived through one personally. What would happen if we actually began to pray? That's the challenge before us now.

# A Life of Worn Out Knees

The Gospel introduces me to this delightful, wonderful life of worn out knees. Jesus says in verse 7, "Ask, and it will be given to you; seek, and you will find; knock and it will be opened to you." It sounds so easy, so simple that we automatically think, "What's the catch, there's got to be a catch?" We think this most because we have all asked for things and heard the door slam on that prayer loud and clear. In fact, if you've walked with Jesus any time at all you know that you don't get everything you ask for just as you have requested. So you may be thinking, "I've prayed and God hasn't answered my prayer, so there has to be a catch. What is it?"

As I study this passage, I do not see where Jesus gives a "catch" here. Do you notice any? Jesus gives no caveat of rule or stipulations. All He says in Scripture is "Ask, and it will be given to you; seek, and you will find; knock, and it will be opened to you." Talk about an incredible promise from God that every person who claims Jesus Christ as Savior should welcome into their life. It's a promise for all of us right here, right now. It's a promise that Jesus is listening and that He is going to move in a mighty way. Besides, prayer is not meant to be so difficult and esoteric that only a few can master it. It's not supposed to be so complex that only those with the highest IQ can enjoy it. Prayer is so wonderful that the smallest child can begin to pray by faith and with those stuttering and stammering lips, the prayer lifts up to God and God hears. Prayer is both wonderful and incredible all rolled into one.

## Knowing Isn't Doing

Tragically, we have a lot of theoretical knowledge about prayer but not a lot of practical doing of prayer. We understand that, in theory, if we as Christians will just pray, God will do something, He will be moved to act on our behalf. In practice, however, we don't pray and therefore don't see God do very much. We understand in theory there is great power in prayer. Because we don't pray as we should, we never realize fully the power we have at our fingertips. So, we understand prayer in theory but we misunderstand prayer in practice.

Again, stop and analyze your prayer life last week. How much time did you spend speaking to God in prayer? How many times did you get on your knees? If you are physically unable to get on your knees, which is okay, how much time did you just bow your head and pray? How much time while driving down the road did you pray, (eyes open, of course)? Or, how much time did you spend journaling your prayers?

It's very easy to be loaded with guilt right now because most of us know without analyzing that we do not pray as we ought. We will spend an average of four hours a day watching television, but many won't spend four minutes in prayer.

The late Martin Lloyd-Jones, former pastor of Westminster Chapel in Buckingham Gate, England sums up our struggle with prayer. He said, "Of all the activities in which the Christian engages and which are part of the Christian life there is surely none which causes so much perplexity and raises so many problems as the activity which we call prayer." He's exactly right.

## Prayer Changes Things

Prayer is so incredible because prayer changes things. Prayer changes circumstances. Prayer changes the hearts of people. Prayer changes the events that come our way. Prayer changes things and yet, we struggle so much in the activity of prayer.

When we grasp the severity of lostness in America, among our friends and family, it should cause us to pray for those who are lost. In a previous chapter, I discussed lostness at length. I poured my heart out about the lostness that's all around us. Understanding what we know about the eternity of lost people, and we fail to be moved to pray for the lost people we encounter, what are we doing? As the body of Christ, are we not supposed to take seriously what God says and begin to pray and do the things that God says in order to see lost people come to Christ? Yes, we are. It's a serious thing. We should have worn out knees. We understand that prayer changes things.

Gypsy Smith understood the power of prayer to change events and lives. He was born March 31, 1860 in Great Britain. When he was 16 years old, he came to know the Lord Jesus and shortly thereafter he was called to be an evangelist. Man, was he ever an evangelist. He preached the Gospel wherever he went. He made dozens of trips from London to America to preach the Gospel because he was burdened for the lostness of America. How incredible is that? He never went to school because he was a gypsy; it wasn't available to him. He had no formal education in the great halls of theology in Europe. One time he shared how his learning had been acquired, "I didn't go through your colleges and seminaries because they wouldn't have me. But I have been to the feet of Jesus where the only true scholarship is learned." In other words, he rested at the feet of Jesus in prayer and he studied at the feet of Jesus for knowledge to carry out the ministry. That's where the truest scholarship is learned.

Gypsy Smith, believed so much in the power of prayer that he began to pray for his Uncle Rodney. He confidently petitioned God, "Father, I know You're going to save Uncle Rodney." But he lived in a time where it would have been impolite and offensive for the younger man to speak directly to his elder about such a sensitive matter. One day, Smith walks up to his Uncle Rodney and the man says to him, "Young man, what is wrong with your pants? You have holes in the knees of your pants while the rest of your outfit looks good. What's wrong with your knees?" Gypsy Smith looked at his uncle and said, "I've been on my knees praying and I've been praying specifically for you that God would save you." And just a few moments later they bowed their heads together and that dear uncle became a Jesus follower that day. Prayer changes things.[9]

## Prayer is Hard Work

Prayer is hard work, is it not? If you don't agree, I promise you, you're not praying enough. Prayer is like doing your daily cardio exercises. You get on the exercise machine and begin to run to get your heart rate up. You keep going and pushing hard. When you begin it is incredibly hard and you probably can't go for long. But over time, muscle strength is built and your heart pumps a greater volume of blood and your lungs don't burn as much. You are stronger.

In the same way, prayer is the spiritual exercise of coming before God,

9   John N. Hamblin, *Fire in the Pulpit* (Murfreesboro, TN: Sword of the Lord, n.d.), 82.

calling out and watching what He is going to do. It is a discipline we must have in our life to get a clear signal from Him. If we don't have the discipline in our life to pray, we will fail in this most critical spiritual area. Jesus' call to prayer demands we develop this most important of disciplines. We must not be deterred for fear of unanswered prayer. Our challenge and calling is simply *to* pray.

It is interesting to note that nowhere in this passage on prayer in Matthew, or in any other teaching of Jesus on prayer, does He ever talk about unanswered prayer. Imagine that! There is no place in the Bible where Jesus specifically says, "Now, listen, when God doesn't answer your prayer, then you need to do this or you need to do that." You can look, but that verse doesn't exist!

Our Lord Jesus knows that every prayer is answered by God the Father, every single prayer. Of course, He may not answer it to our liking, but God the Father answers every prayer we pray. You may have prayed about something for a long time and been left wondering, "When is God going to answer? When is He going to respond?" Perhaps He already has. Perhaps He's said, "You know I don't think that's a good thing for you, therefore, I don't want that in your life." It's possible and our sovereign God should be allowed to do that. Maybe He has done that in prayers you have been praying.

Jesus never speaks of unanswered prayer; He knows every prayer is answered. Instead, the Lord challenges us to pray and ask His Father for what we need. Later in the New Testament, James, the half-brother of Jesus, tells us that we miss out on receiving from God because we don't pray. James 4:2-3 says, "You do not have, because you do not ask. You ask and do not receive, because you ask wrongly to spend it on your passions." James is telling us that we do not have because we don't ask *or* because we ask with wrong motive. When our motives are selfish and egocentric, it's very likely we will either hear a resounding "No!" from God or dead silence. It is therefore essential we analyze our motives in prayer. That does not, however, dismiss the fact that Jesus still tells us to ask, seek and knock.

As I've said, there is no greater power on the face of the earth than prayer. I know, when preachers say things like that some respond, "Oh come on! How can that be?" I know I'm right when I make this statement: There is no greater power on the face of the earth than when a believer in Jesus

Christ falls before God in prayer. There is something exceedingly strong and powerful when this occurs. For this reason, William Cowper's old and poetic line is true, *"Satan trembles when he sees the weakest saint upon his knees."* Why not stop right now and begin the process of wearing out your knees by committing to a life of devoted prayer? You'll never be sorry you did!

# Persevering On My Knees

The one thing I have learned in my own prayer life is that effective prayer requires perseverance. Because prayer is hard work and a discipline demanding to be developed, it is easy to let the call to prayer slip. We must persevere if we are going to see God moved to action by our prayers.

## A Command to Persevere

Jesus says, "Ask, and it will be given to you; seek, and you will find; knock and it will be opened to you." The three words – ask, seek, knock – escalate in intensity. They are imperatives from our Lord Jesus. We understand an imperative as a command. It's like when my mother issued me a command to take out the trash, "Byron, I'm telling you, (commanding you) to do this right now!" So Jesus commands that we come before God and ask Him, seek Him, and knock through prayer. These are not just run-of-the-mill commands from Jesus. They are present imperatives in the Greek language.

In the language of the New Testament there are two different kinds of imperatives, the "aorist" and the "present." Let me explain this to you and while I do it, I'll do some marital counseling for those of you who may be struggling in your marriage.

The *aorist imperative* is a command to be carried out at a distinct point in time. It could go something like this for those struggling in their marriage. When wanting to go to sleep, the husband looks at his wife and barks, "Turn out the light." That's an aorist imperative. When in an argument he yells, "Keep your mouth shut." That's another aorist imperative. When he comes home hungry from work he commands, "Bring me my dinner." Yes, you got it, another aorist imperative. At this point, his bride has had all she can take so she pushes divorce papers across the table towards him and issues her own aorist imperative, "Sign the papers." All of these are specific commands to be carried out at one point in time. Does that make sense? I hope so. And, by the way, I pray this does not describe the way you treat your spouse.

Using the same poor example let me show the difference between aorist and *present imperatives*. A present imperative is not to be carried out at a single point in time, it has continuous action. The husband would tell his wife, "Keep turning out that light. Keep shutting your mouth. Keep bringing me my dinner." To which she would say, "Keep signing those papers." You get it? That is a present imperative meaning that it has continuous action. It is a command with continuous action attached to it. And this is what Jesus seeks to convey to us. Jesus is saying, "Don't just ask but keep on asking. Don't just seek, but keep on seeking. Don't just knock, but keep on knocking."

## Dependence and Prayer

Prayer is a statement of my dependence upon God. If we are honest, most people pray little until an urgent need in their life arises. When a major crisis hits up close and personal, that's when most learn to pray. At that time we ask and keep on asking, seek and keep on seeking, and knock and keep on knocking! Until then, especially living in abundant-laden America where we honestly have very few "needs" that weigh heavily upon us, we oftentimes don't ask, seek or knock. We don't have the need for God to provide daily bread because our local supermarket has done that. We usually have at least an okay car to drive and a good roof over our head. We don't have many needs or threats that cause our life to hang in the balance and for that I'm thankful. Because this is so, we can easily fall into a trap of failing to persevere in prayer.

I'm not saying we do not have need to bring everything to God in prayer. This need applies to all of us. In fact, because we can go to the supermarket and not worry about where our next meal comes from, and because we can crank our car and move around town, and because we have a good roof to sleep under at night, isn't this all the more reason why we should pray? Shouldn't we thank God with more determination for what He has already given us? First Thessalonians 5:18 tells us to "give thanks in all circumstances." We should never be guilty of taking for granted that which God has so richly blessed us. Regardless of our lack of present need, our thankfulness in prayer proclaims our dependence upon our God.

When great need does arise, however, these become special times of declaring our dependence upon God in prayer. Many of us can remember a time when we've been so financially distraught that we desperately needed God to introduce Himself to our bank account. Every young couple I've met, unless Mommy and Daddy are helping them out, arrives here at some point. I know I've been there, begging God to show up on my family's behalf to grant even a small financial blessing. It's an area of dependence when we come before God and say, "God, in my finances I'm hurting and I need some help and I'm asking You to help me."

How about the car you drive? Have you ever found yourself praying that God would keep it running because you don't have the funds for repairs and didn't want to walk to work? I've been there and it's not fun. Then again, I did find it an opportunity to persevere in prayer and believe God would meet all of my family's needs.

When my family moved from Houston to a very rural area in Southeast Texas for me to pastor my first church, we loaded up and headed out on faith and prayer. We had faith God would provide the financial shortage we knew we would have every month. I had been working as an accountant for one of the largest oil companies in the world when God called us to leave and go into fulltime ministry. The only problem was that He didn't bring my large salary along as part of the deal. We cranked the moving van and relocated by faith. The prayer aspect of our journey came into play each and every month as we sought God to make up the routine financial shortfall. Like I say, it was a matter of faith coupled with prayer.

A few months into the new work, I was struggling more than a little with worry and doubt. I know, preachers are not supposed to worry, I get that. But the grind of learning to pastor effectively coupled with daily financial strain was taking its toll on me. I received a call early one week requesting me to preach at a nursing home about 20 miles from my church. I had spoken there a couple of other times but this time I was snowed under with sermon preparation and other ministry demands and felt I did not have the time. Reluctantly, I told the old gentleman on the phone he needed to get someone else. The following Monday he called again. Unable to find a preacher, he asked if I would reconsider. Again, I assured him that my week was too busy and I would not be able to speak. Looking back after so many years in ministry, I confess that this was not a high point in my calling as a servant of the Lord. The old fellow realized he wasn't getting anywhere so we hung up and went about our business. The next morning he called for the third time and asked that I come that Thursday. This time I was beginning to feel a little like young Samuel with Eli telling him that the Lord was trying to speak to him. I confirmed that I would see him Thursday at 11:00.

What I haven't told you was that I was driving a car that had no working air conditioner. The air had not blown – neither cold nor hot – in over a year and it was hot outside to say the least. The heat and humidity in Southeast Texas in July is so intense that you can almost hear the sap in the pine trees popping and bubbling under the bark. The dirt roads are so hot that even the dogs walk quickly across in the heat of the day. To say that it is merely hot is an understatement of epic proportion and I desperately wanted to find enough extra money to fix the A/C in my car. With all the other demands we had, I knew that wasn't happening.

When I left that Thursday morning it was already steaming at 10:30. I climbed into the car, rolled down the windows, loosened my tie and headed to the nursing home. By the time I reached my destination my hair was blown crazy and sweat was rolling down my back. I parked, rolled up the windows, tightened my tie, put on my jacket, grabbed my Bible and locked my car doors. I was sweaty but I was also ready to share a word of encouragement with these dear people.

It was a marvelous morning! Those precious people loved on me more than I deserved and I preached to them the joys awaiting us when we enter the gates of Heaven. We sang some old hymns to an out of tune piano and closed in a special time of prayer. It was a blessing and I was ashamed that it had taken three requests before I had sense enough to say "Yes."

As I walked back to my car, it was near 12:00 p.m. on my watch. The sun was high and the breeze was hiding. I took my jacket off, hanging it on the hook in the back, rolled down the windows and cranked my car to head home. At that moment I felt impressed from deep within to turn on my air conditioner. I chuckled because I knew that was pointless. It hadn't worked in so many months that there were probably spiders nesting deep inside the condenser. Again, I felt the prompting to try my air conditioner. *Just turn it on. Give it a shot.* I reached down to the fan button and in one quick move turned it onto high. At that moment the coldest air that had ever come forth from the vents in that little car began to blow. It was like a West Texas gusher of oil, only it was clear, cold air gushing forth like it had not done in well over a year. I was floored! And then I heard that still small voice speak softly but directly to my heart. It said, "Byron, what have you been so worried about? As long as you do as I ask you, I will always take care of you and provide for your needs!" Message delivered; message received!

What God was telling me at that moment were the words just preceding Jesus's comments on prayer in Mathew chapter 7. With loud speaker clarity God was saying, "But seek first the kingdom of God and His righteousness, and all these things will be added to you." I was never supposed to worry or doubt, these being a declaration of independence from God. Instead, God sought my dependence upon Him in prayer. He longed for me to seek Him first, above all else, even the heavy demands of ministry. And what did He promise? That my dependence upon Him would never be wasted but would always pay great dividends!

Do you think it was just a coincidence that my A/C worked that day? I hope not! That was a divine moment when the amazing God who loves us showed up to answer my prayers just because He could. What's even better, as I look back through the years, is the knowledge that even if I'd driven home in the heat, the next time I received a call to come preach at the nursing home I would not have hesitated to say "Yes!" And by the way, my air conditioner stayed fixed for the next five years of driving that car. As my wife always says, "What God fixes, He fixes!"

## Call to Me!

When Jesus says to ask, He wants us to keep on asking. When He says to seek, we must keep on seeking. And when He says we are to knock, we are to keep on knocking. It is all part of God's great plan whereby He instructs His dependent children to call out to Him. A verse that has meant so much to me is Jeremiah 33:3, "Call to me and I will answer you, and will tell you great and hidden things that you have not known."

When God says, "Call to me," it is like standing on the corner in New York City and hailing a taxi cab. The weak and timid often find themselves walking because the person who shouts the loudest grabs the cab drivers attention. In similar fashion God tells us to shout out to Him, to hail Him with boldness and perseverance. It is relentlessly pursuing God in prayer until He answers and shows you the great and hidden things you are crying out to understand.

The same principle can be seen in how I trained my children to respond to my whistle when they were small. When I was in high school, I taught myself how to whistle very loud. I'd always been able to whistle a tune, but this was the kind of whistle a referee in a football game needs to make. Loud and obnoxious! My kids will tell you that nobody they know can whistle louder than their daddy, (I take that as a point of pride by the way!). When our babies were playing away from the house in the evening, I could step outside and whistle in the twilight and in just moments I'd see their little legs carrying them lickity-split across the grass headed home. If we were at a ballgame and they were on the field, when I whistled you would see their heads pop up looking for Dad. Why? They knew my whistle and always responded when they heard it rolling through the air. That's what God is saying He will do when we cry out to Him. "Call to me and *I will answer you!*"

## Knock-on!

Jesus says to "Knock and keep on knocking. Don't stop knocking whatever you do and it will be opened to you." He's not giving us an encouragement to knock as long as we feel like it. He's telling us to just do it. We are to ask. We are to seek. We are to knock. And we are to keep on asking, seeking and knocking until God answers. That is perseverance in prayer. If we won't persevere in prayer, we will quit. We will give up. We make the determination that the prayers we are praying are not working and we'll stop. Think of what there is to lose if you stop. Most likely you are very cloudy on the perfect plan of God regarding what you are bringing before Him in prayer. That is all the more reason why you must persevere. How do you know that the next time you pray about that which you've prayed about a thousand times before will not be the moment when the heart of God is moved to respond to your request? Perseverance is the key! Ask, seek and knock in perseverance and leave the results to God.

Jonathon Goforth was a missionary to China. Upon arrival in that distant far Eastern land, Goforth was mentored by the great Hudson Taylor. Taylor was the founder of the China Inland Mission. At the time he died there were over 700 preaching stations across China proclaiming the

Gospel. China still feels the positive impact today of Taylor's work so many years ago. As Hudson Taylor sat down with Jonathon Goforth to impart wisdom for serving God in China, he gave him the key to his successful ministry. Taylor said, "You must move forward on your knees. If you're going to move forward at all, you must move forward on your knees." This veteran missionary of the Gospel understood that apart from everything else, if you're going to have success, you will do so primarily through prayer. You've got to move forward on your knees. You ask, you seek, and you knock from a kneeling position.

I mentioned earlier that we are in need of a spiritual awakening in America. I am convicted that God is watching and waiting for the evangelical churches in America to not stand tall in self-sufficiency but to bow low in dependence. He is not looking for polish, He's checking our posture! The reason we do not have awakening is not because God does not desire to flood this land with His presence. We do not have awakening because we are churches that have found little need for God to be successful in our own eyes. We know how to sing moving songs and communicate with a conversational style so well that He isn't expected to show up. It's as if the God of creation has been told to take a seat and we'll get back to you when the time is right. There is no doubt that with current technology we have more opportunity to reach this world with the Gospel than ever. We are simply too unwilling to bow the knee and persevere in prayer.

## Confidence on My Knees

I said earlier that Jesus never mentions the possibility of unanswered prayer. Instead, what we are given next in Matthew's Gospel is one of the most encouraging verses in the Bible to fuel our confidence in prayer. Jesus says in verse eight, "For everyone who asks receives, and the one who seeks finds, and to the one who knocks it will be opened." It's as if Jesus says, "If you have a problem, just ask God, just seek God in perseverance, just keep on knocking and the door will be opened to you!" When He says *everyone*, He is referencing all Jesus followers. Prayer is for all who have acknowledged by faith that Christ is the Son of the living God. What an incredible promise from God to everyone who believes in His Son.

## No Useful Moves Detected

When I have time to kill, you may find me playing the solitaire application on my iPhone. I enjoy this game because one overlooked move can spell the difference between winning and losing. To help the player out, the designer programmed the game with a "hint" icon that can be turned on or off. Whenever my eyes are having trouble focusing on the rows of cards, I can tap the "hint" icon to find out if any available moves have been overlooked. When there are no moves to report, the device reads "No Useful Moves Detected."

God has designed us with an internal source that helps us determine whether the moves we make are useful or not. He is called the Holy Spirit and He gives us "hints" to assist us in walking with Him in obedience because you cannot pray with confidence when you are not walking with God in obedience. Let that sink in deep; this is gold. You can't pray effectively when you're not walking with God in obedience. When you are walking in disobedience, the Holy Spirit says to our heart, "No Useful Moves Detected." This conviction we feel is God's way of telling us to turn back to the straight and narrow. You cannot pray with confidence when your heart is not devoted fully to God. For some of you this is the precise reason your time in prayer falls flat and has no zip or power. You are walking down a road where there are "No Useful Moves Detected" and you need to turn back.

In 1 John 3:21-22 the Bible says, "Beloved, if our hearts do not condemn us, we have confidence before God; and whatever we ask we receive from Him, because we keep His commandments and do what pleases Him." Do you see the necessity of obedience spelled out in these verses? It's crucial to walk in obedience to God's commands so that our hearts do not condemn us and we lose confidence before God.

A life of obedience should lead us to pray with confidence. God confirms this to us in 1 John 5:14-15 where the Bible says, "And this is the confidence we have toward Him, that if we ask anything according to His will He hears us. And if we know that He hears us in whatever we ask, we know that we have the requests that we have asked of Him." Powerful prayer comes from an obedient life.

Prayer is also found to be most effective when done from a heart warmed through sincere daily devotion to Jesus. Our confidence level increases as we spend time with God. When we open the Word of God and begin to read, our hearts are turned towards Him. Then, when we get down on our knees and begin to pray, we realize that God cares about the particular burdens we carry. Of the more than seven billion people on the face of the earth, God cares about each person's prayers individually. The more we pray and our level of devotion rises, the more our confidence in God's willingness to answer rises also. We begin to truly believe that God will answer the prayers we pray. That's the confidence the Bible tells is available to those who walk closely with God.

Have you ever walked so close behind someone that you step on the back of their foot and their shoe comes off? Usually you know it because they turn and give you the evil eye for invading their personal space. From a spiritual angle, are you following so closely after God in your daily devotion that when you being to pray it's as if He says, "You stepped on my shoe again because you're following so close in my footsteps." The person who follows God like that is assured of having a confident prayer life.

When our youngest daughter, Raegan, was seven, she and I were Christmas shopping at the local mall. As we walked out of one store and into the stream of people moving by, my little girl circled around behind me to come up on my left side. As she did our legs got tangled and she walked on the back of my legs. You can probably guess what happened next. In front of hundreds of Christmas shoppers, we face planted on the ground for everyone to see. It was a spectacular demonstration of falling in a crowded mall! We were both embarrassed because you can't cover up something as drastic as two people sprawling on the floor amid shopping bags and shuffling feet. Just as quickly as we fell, we jumped up, faces flush with humiliation. Since that night, I have related this to my walk with God on many occasions. Because I was carrying our packages with my right hand, my baby girl was positioning herself to walk as closely as possible with her daddy and hold my hand on the left. While I know it is impossible to trip God, I want to position myself right up under His feet so that I can walk closely with Him and hold His hand through life. Don't you?

## Guarantee of Time Well Spent

Because I have embraced the Gospel and am following after Jesus Christ, I have been guaranteed by God that the time spent on my knees in prayer is not wasted time. It is guaranteed to have a productive impact for God's Kingdom. I can prove this to be true in Scripture.

In Matthew 7:9-10, Jesus uses an illustration to prove His point. He says, "Or which one of you, if his son asks him for bread, will give him a stone? Or if he asks for fish, will give him a serpent?" Jesus is using an outrageously absurd illustration to make His point regarding the guarantees we have in prayer. I think He was looking at the fathers seated before Him and tied His sermon on prayer down with a powerful illustration they weren't soon to forget. In essence Jesus said, "You daddies sitting before me, which one of you if your son walks up to you and said, 'Father, I'm really hungry. Can I have a piece of bread?' that you're going to reach down and give him a rock and say, 'Hey son, crunch on this for a while.' Or if your son comes up to you and says, 'Daddy, I'm about to starve, can I have a piece of fish?' Which of you dads would turn around, grab a snake off the ground and hand it to your son saying, 'Nope, you take the snake instead.'" This scenario wouldn't happen, would it?

Through this purposefully absurd illustration, Jesus is helping us make an important connection. He is saying that since we love our children so much that we wouldn't dare do something as ridiculous to them as this, then we should never doubt that God the Father has our best interest at heart when we seek Him in prayer. This is confirmed in verse 11 where Jesus says, "If you then, who are evil, know how to give good gifts to your children, how much more will your Father who is in Heaven give good gifts to those who ask Him!" There's our guarantee that God will always give us what is good for us when we pray.

I would never say that God is honor bound to grant my selfish wishes. But when we pray for that which is good for us and will benefit His Kingdom, He will always answer in a way that is pleasing to us, guaranteed.

For example, if you were to pray, "God, my prayer is that You help me to grow as a believer. As a disciple of Jesus, help me to grow so that I can help others to come to know who Jesus Christ is," then it's guaranteed He will answer that prayer in the affirmative.

## God never gives me something evil when I pray.

He will not give me anything evil when I pray. He'll never turn to me when my stomach is growling and say, "Go crunch some rocks." Or, "here's a snake for you." He's not going to do it because He is not evil.

## God guarantees to never make a mistake in answering my prayer.

God never makes a mistake. No person has ever heard God say, "Oops," because He never has. Every earthly parent makes mistakes, but not God. I've made many parenting mistakes through the years. But God the Father will never make a mistake. Regardless of how I think He should have answered, if God says "no" to my prayer, it was not a mistake. It was designed for my protection. I've prayed some prayers a long time, seeking God to answer the way I've wanted. But all I heard was a continual string of "no, no, no." In my human reasoning, I've stood back and thought, *I don't understand why You would say no to this. It's not a bad thing.* But yet, I still hear "no." If I truly believe that my sovereign God loves me greatly and that He can never make a mistake, then why can I not accept the "no" when it comes my way in prayer? Why would I not believe Him and take Him at His word and simply say, "Okay, God, I trust You. I confess a lack of understanding, but that will not make me doubt your goodness." God promises. He guarantees to never make a mistake.

## God will always give me good gifts when I pray.

While I may not understand fully at the moment, I rest in the knowledge that everything that comes from the hand of God is ultimately a good gift for me. That's what Jesus says in verse 11, "If you then, who are evil, know how to give good gifts to your children, how much more will your Father who is in heaven give good things to those who ask Him!" God gives good gifts!

The greatest gift God has ever given is His only Son, simply Jesus. Through the Gospel, He has made salvation available to every person who calls upon the name of Jesus by faith. That's the best gift of all!

# chapter 9
## PURSUIT

"In the first book, O Theophilus, I have dealt with all that Jesus began to do and teach, until the day when He was taken up, after He had given commands through the Holy Spirit to the apostles whom He had chosen. He presented Himself alive to them after His suffering by many proofs, appearing to them during forty days and speaking about the Kingdom of God.

And while staying with them He ordered them not to depart from Jerusalem, but to wait for the promise of the Father, which, He said, 'you heard from me; for John baptized with water, but you will be baptized with the Holy Spirit not many days from now.'

So when they had come together, they asked Him, 'Lord, will you at this time restore the Kingdom to Israel?' He said to them, 'It is not for you to know times or seasons that the Father has fixed by his own authority. But you will receive power when the Holy Spirit has come upon you, and you will be my witnesses in Jerusalem and in all Judea and Samaria, and to the end of the earth.' And when He had said these things, as they were looking on, He was lifted up, and a cloud took Him out of their sight. And while they were gazing into heaven as He went, behold, two men stood by them in white robes, and said, 'Men of Galilee, why do you stand looking into heaven? This Jesus, who was taken up from you into heaven, will come in the same way as you saw Him go into heaven.'"

Acts 1:1-11

ONE SUMMER AT THE FIRST church I pastored, we had a group of 25 or so students go to camp. When they arrived home some of the parents and I met them in the church parking lot to welcome them back. After the crowd disbursed, I asked my student pastor how things went. Paul looked at me with an amazed look on his face and said it went fantastic. He said, "Pastor, out of the group that went we had almost two dozen give their life to Christ." I'm now the one with the amazed look on my face as I wondered if I had heard correctly. We were awestruck at the work of God!

My student pastor went on to say that what had occurred was truly awesome, but hard to understand. He explained that the majority of the students had made a profession of faith in Christ before and most had even been baptized. Now he was wondering why so many were making another profession of faith. And to top it all off, the high school age daughter of the former pastor of the church was one who again professed a first time legitimate faith in Jesus Christ.

Had she never heard the Gospel? Of course she had. I know her father and I know the type messages he had preached for years. She had most definitely been exposed to hundreds of sermons where the plan of salvation had been presented. And yet, now she proclaims that she has finally heard the Gospel message and become a believer. Of course I'm praying, "God, why do things like this happen? What gives?"

## Ears to Hear and Eyes to See

Have you ever wondered why some people quickly "get it" in church and some people don't? Why do some reach out and grab the Gospel from the onset, while for others the message just zips right on by? We've been careful to see how God makes the Gospel available to everyone. While not dismissing the sovereignty of God in salvation, I've also sought to show the responsibility of man. So why do some leave the message hanging and never act upon the good news they've heard?

It appears that some have ears to hear and some do not. Some have eyes to see, while others are blind. This, of course, is proven as biblical when you read passages like Isaiah 6. When this Old Testament prophet was commissioned by God to advance against the darkness, God gave him a message that proves what I seek to convey. In Isaiah 6:9-10 the Bible says, "And [God] said, 'Go, and say to this people: Keep on hearing, but do not understand; keep on seeing, but do not perceive. Make the heart of this people dull, and their ears heavy, and blind their eyes; lest they see with their eyes, and hear with their ears, and understand with their hearts, and turn and be healed.'"

Jesus speaks similar truth in the Gospels. In Matthew 23, His harshest words were spoken to the teachers of the Law and Pharisees. He called them hypocrites, blind guides, white-washed tombs filled with dead man's bones. In Matthew 23:15, Jesus says, "Woe to you, teachers of the Law and Pharisees, you hypocrites! You shut the Kingdom of Heaven in men's faces. You yourselves do not enter, nor will you let those enter who are trying to." These are exceedingly strong words against those who have ears but can't hear and eyes but cannot see.

We have come to the final chapter. We have looked at the Gospel in detail. It really is simply all about Jesus Christ! Simply Jesus! The question I place before you now is really very simple too: *Do you have ears to hear and eyes to see?*

# The Big Story

We have established that the Gospel is the greatest news ever to bless planet Earth. It is God's larger-than-life metanarrative shouting to all that He is here and redemption is available. The big story of God weaves like a golden thread through all 66 books of the Bible and is seen in the myriad of real life events revealed on the pages of Scripture. Each little piece of God's story fits perfectly together in the overall big story of God and His unveiling of Himself to us. His big story tells us that He is here and wants a relationship. We don't have to die in our sin and suffer wrath for eternity. God has paved the way to forgiveness through the Gospel message and there is salvation through Jesus Christ, the Son of God!

Dave Harvey says it like this, "The Gospel is the heart of the Bible.

Everything in Scripture is either preparation for the Gospel, presentation of the Gospel, or participation in the Gospel."[10] He's exactly right.

The Gospel is the good news that Jesus Christ came, that he died, that he rose again and is alive today, and if you place your faith and trust in Him, you can have the glorious gift of eternal life. Your sins will be forgiven through the mercy and grace of God.

We've seen that the Gospel is God's preplanned answer to evil found in this world. When you see the huge proliferation of evil today, you must know that it has not caught God by surprise. In eternity past God the Father developed His plan to conquer evil through the Gospel of His Son.

The Gospel is the battle cry that summons the forces of good to rise against the forces of evil. In many ways on this side of eternity, it is a summons to prayer, a call to stand firm and overcome all that seeks to destroy our spiritual peace. When we pray and stand firm upon the Word, the power of the Gospel is seen in our conviction and beliefs, thus Jesus is glorified.

Many search for answers all their life but because they do not have ears to hear or eyes to see, they come up short. The Gospel is the final solution to the sin problem that haunts us deep inside. Many reject the Gospel, unwilling to bare their soul before a Holy God with utter truthfulness. As a result of pride, the Gospel is allowed to slip past with no eternal change transpiring.

God's absolute and total plan for the advancement of the Kingdom of Jesus is also contained in the Gospel. It is His plan for the advancement of the Kingdom of His Son. Because the Gospel originates with God, it is a perfect plan; it is a divine plan. You and I cannot enhance the Gospel with anything. There's nothing we can do to make the Gospel better. It is the greatest news already, perfect in every way. It cannot be improved upon by anything we do or do not do. God's Gospel is perfect!

We can stand in the way of the Gospel, opposing it by our actions, but we cannot make or define the Gospel better than what God has already done. It is always good news! Our challenge as Jesus followers is to advance the Kingdom of God on this earth by spreading the good news of the Gospel in our circles of influence.

---

10    Matt Chandler, *The Explicit Gospel* (Wheaton, IL: Crossway, 2012), 11.

# The Kingdom of Jesus

The Kingdom of Jesus is the Kingdom of God. Whenever a reference in the Bible is made to the Kingdom of Heaven, the Kingdom of God or the Kingdom of Jesus it should be understood that we are talking about only one Kingdom. While we worship a triune God consisting of Father, Son and Holy Spirit, they are One. We do not worship three distinct gods; we worship One God in three persons. Therefore, because the Godhead is completely One, there can be only one Kingdom.

You might ask, "Do we worship all three – Father, Son and Holy Spirit?" The answer is certainly "yes," because while all three have distinct roles, they are nonetheless still One God. We worship the Father because the Father is God. We worship Jesus because the Son is God. We worship the Holy Spirit because He is God too. So when we talk about the Kingdom of God, it is synonymous with the Kingdom of Jesus.

In John 10:30, Jesus was accused of blasphemy by the Jewish leaders for saying, "I and the Father are one." In other words, "We are inseparable. We are one complete unit." When you've seen Jesus, you've seen God. This is anything but blasphemy; it is correct theology.

When the Bible references the Kingdom of God, it is acceptable to say the Kingdom of Jesus, because Jesus is King! Perhaps you've sung the lyrics of Matthew Bridges' hymn before…

> *Crown Him with many crowns, the Lamb upon His throne.*
> *Hark! How the heavenly anthem drowns all music but its own.*
> *Awake, my soul, and sing of Him who died for thee,*
> *And hail Him as thy matchless King through all eternity.*

Praise God for His Son, the King of kings and Lord of lords. When we arrive in Heaven we will bow before a throne with King Jesus seated upon it. Time will be no more as we celebrate Him in worship beyond our most creative imaginations. We will worship the King in His Kingdom for eternity.

# The Message of the Son of God

When Jesus walked this earth, He was the living, breathing personification of the Gospel. John 1 verses 1 and 14 says, "In the beginning was the Word, and the Word was with God, and the Word was God. And the Word became flesh and dwelt among us, and we have seen His glory, glory as of the only Son from the Father, full of grace and truth." Jesus, in every way, was good news then, and He is good news today. He brought a message of salvation. Good news! He told how captives would be set free. Good news! He made it clear that through believing in Him, your sins could be forgiven, and you would not suffer an eternity in hell. That is good news. He made all of this very clear because it is good news. Jesus is the only one who has walked this earth that is truly "not of this world."

In some way, every teaching of the Lord Jesus Christ, regardless of the topic he spoke about, was a delivery of the Gospel. When Jesus talked about the seed that fell on the path, He was talking about the Word of God and the embracing of His Gospel. When Jesus explained deep truths or spoke in parables, He was communicating the Gospel because everything He said was a message of good news to those who would simply hear. When Jesus Christ, who is truth personified, began to speak, the good news came forth, which was and is the Gospel message.

When Jesus taught about the Kingdom, He did so from a position of power. He was not nervous or fearful by the evil threatening His Kingdom. He knew His Father's plan would ultimately and decisively deal a fatal blow to the enemy. When Jesus arose from the dead, He validated every claim He made by His resurrection. That is exceedingly great news!

In Acts 1:3, Luke, the writer of Acts, says that Jesus "...presented Himself alive to them after His suffering by many proofs, appearing to them during forty days and speaking about the Kingdom of God." First, this is good news because Jesus is alive. As the old hymn goes, "I serve a risen Savior, He's in the world today. I know that He is living, whatever men may say." Jesus is alive, and He gave "many proofs of himself, appearing to them." The Bible talks of Jesus appearing to over 500 at one time in 1 Corinthians 15. So in verse three, Jesus is both alive and making His presence known.

Jesus is also speaking. He is "...speaking about the Kingdom of God." For forty days, the risen King gave a crystal clear message delivered from the imperial palace, regarding the Kingdom of God. It was the same message He had been preaching for the past three years; a message about His Kingdom. In Mark 1:14-15 it says, "Now after John was arrested, Jesus came into Galilee, proclaiming the Gospel of God, and saying, 'The time is fulfilled, and the Kingdom of God is at hand; repent and believe in the Gospel.'" Here, Jesus is unveiling the closeness, the nearness, the at-hand presence, of the Kingdom of God.

It must have been an electric moment when Jesus entered the synagogue in Nazareth on the Sabbath and He stood to read from the scroll of Isaiah. The Bible says in Luke 4:16-19, "And He came to Nazareth, where He had been brought up. And as was his custom, He went to the synagogue on the Sabbath day, and He stood up to read. And the scroll of the prophet Isaiah was given to Him. He unrolled the scroll and found the place where it was written, 'The Spirit of the Lord is upon me, because He has anointed me to proclaim good news to the poor. He has sent me to proclaim liberty to the captives and recovering of sight to the blind, to set at liberty those who are oppressed, to proclaim the year of the Lord's favor.'" Again we find an example of Jesus proclaiming the Gospel message and good news to the poor.

The most powerful moment that day, however, was when Jesus finished reading, rolled up the scroll and sat down. Jesus then looked at the men in the room and in verse 21 says, "Today this Scripture has been fulfilled in your hearing." What an electric, high voltage moment in time! The long awaited Messiah had just declared Himself in the hearing of those attending the synagogue that day. The Kingdom of Jesus is the message spoken of by the Son of God throughout the Word of God. You see it over and over and over. The message has never changed!

## The Prize to be Sought Above All Else

The pursuit of the Kingdom of Jesus should trump every other desire in our life. In Matthew 6:33, Jesus says that we are to "seek first the Kingdom of God and His righteousness, and all these things will be added to you." Jesus confronts those whose minds are fixed on temporal matters and the kingdoms of this earth. Not unlike today, the people He spoke to ran from place-to-place searching for clothing and food and drink. They could not fathom how they would acquire enough money to have all their needs met; they were consumed with clothing, money and food or the lack of these material things.

But Jesus boils their never-ending worry and searching down to one verse designed to instruct all of us in what is most important. Jesus told them to quit searching after the things of this world, but seek Him and His Kingdom above all else and then they would find everything they could want or need. Many people struggle because the very last item on their priority list is Jesus.

People seek after anything and everything for answers but the Kingdom of God. We treasure worldly opinion on how to live stable and happy lives, but apart from the Kingdom of God, it can never last. Jesus is not encouraging us to seek a political or geographical kingdom on this earth that cannot satisfy. But He is adamant about seeking the only Kingdom that will make the total difference in our lives and that is His Kingdom. We are told to absolutely seek first the Kingdom of God and then, only then, will we find what we really crave deep inside.

The Kingdom of God must be the first priority in the life of the Jesus follower. Only when it is can we can claim the promise from Jesus that "…all these things will be added to you as well." Is that not a splendid promise from God? In essence He's saying, "If you will seek first my Kingdom, I'll remove the worry that consumes you. I'll take the burden of loneliness from off your back. I will take away your sin when you confess me, and you will not carry the weight of guilt anymore." That is an incredible promise of God, is it not? That's part of the Gospel message, a prize to be sought above everything else.

Erwin Lutzer, senior pastor of Moody Church in Chicago, says, "When we seek first the Kingdom of God and His righteousness, fulfillment comes as a by-product of our love for God. And that satisfaction is better than we ever imagined. God can make the pieces of this world's puzzle fit together; he helps us view the world from a new perspective." That's what God does.

Many people have so misplaced their priorities that seeking God's Kingdom first is an abstract idea they can't process. When I say many, I include great multitudes of people who claim a relationship with Christ in that category. We want God's presence. We desire His assistance. But if we're honest, many must admit that the God they beseech so fervently during times of trouble drops off their priority list once the yellow caution flag has lifted. Oh, we may confess that we love Jesus, but our priorities cry out against our confession. If this describes you, why would you ever expect "all these things shall be added unto you?" Why would you expect that when the pattern of your life relegates God to less than first place? The Gospel is so incredible, that we should desire to seek the Kingdom of God with diligence all our life.

Sir Edmund Hillary was the first man to stand on top of the world. He and his Nepalese Sherpa, Tenzing Norgay, accomplished this goal on May 29, 1953 when they ascended the final difficult steps up the 29,029 feet of Mount Everest. It was his life ambition to conquer this great mountain. Later, Hillary said, "Despite all I have seen and experienced, I still get the same simple thrill out of glimpsing a tiny patch of snow in a high mountain gully and feel the same urge to climb towards it." Should we do less when it comes to our pursuit of God? Why do we climb toward the kingdom's we can build on this earth with great gusto but neglect the only Kingdom that ultimately matters and will last for eternity?

I think of Robert Peary, who claimed to lead the first expedition to the North Pole, arriving on April 6, 1909. What was inside of this man that drove him to weather the unbearable to accomplish his goal? What was left behind by him other than some lettering on a page or a few quotes easily found on the internet? Why do we not pursue the Kingdom of God like Peary's pursuit of the North Pole? We have an inheritance awaiting us that far surpasses the mysteries of the polar ice cap.

The life goal of Robert Ballard was to find the *Titanic*. He spent 13 years relentlessly pursuing his dream. When he found it, he wrote these words in his personal journal. "My first direct view of *Titanic* lasted less than two minutes, but the stark sight of her immense black hull towering above the ocean floor will remain forever ingrained in my memory. My lifelong dream was to find this great ship, and during the past thirteen years the quest for her had dominated my life. Now, finally, the quest was over." Throughout his 13-year quest, Ballard took 53,000 photographs and spent vast sums of money before he found *Titanic*. That was the great quest, the grand goal and dream of his life.

We can do better as the Church of the Lord Jesus Christ. Our quest must have more substance than finding a sunken sea vessel made by men whose pride caused them to think it unsinkable. We can do better than Hillary,

Peary and Ballard in our search for a real Kingdom that will last forever. We must do better!

Describe your pursuit of the Kingdom of God. How are you pursuing the Kingdom? What characterizes your daily life and pursuit of God? How would you describe it? Would you have the same fearlessness of Sir Edmund Hillary, the courage of Robert Peary, or the amazing perseverance of Robert Ballard? What would you journal about your pilgrimage towards the Kingdom of God? Could it go like this?

> "My first glimpse of *salvation* and the Kingdom of God has lasted me all of these many years, and the stark sight of the immensity of the glorious Gospel of Jesus Christ has stood above everything else from that moment forward. My knowledge that the blood of Christ has covered my sins is deeply ingrained in my heart and memory in such a way that I cannot get over it. The daily goal of my life has been to follow after God, to seek Him first. It is the quest of my life and I will not be content until I kneel in His magnificent presence in the Kingdom of Heaven."

What if we pursued the Kingdom of God like that? Truly we would find that "all these things shall be added unto you." Because of what God did in providing the Gospel, a quest of this magnitude is not only possible, it is expected!

## Life and Great Expectation

The Kingdom of Jesus is a Kingdom of life and great expectation. It's not a Kingdom of death, with nothing to look forward to other than a dark grave. It is a Kingdom of life because the Gospel is all about life! God answers our questions regarding death, but He doesn't camp out on this sad topic; God is firmly on the side of life. Isn't that a cool thing?

That's how God portrays this to us, that the Gospel is the good news of the Kingdom of the Lord Jesus Christ. The good news - the death, the burial, and the resurrection - the life of Jesus Christ, that's the Gospel. Remember Luke says in verse 3, "Jesus presented himself alive to them after his suffering by many proofs, appearing to them during forty days and speaking about the Kingdom of God."

Can you imagine being a Jesus follower during that forty day period of time? If there's ever a time I would like to have sat at the feet of Jesus, it would have been the forty day period between the resurrection and the ascension of the Lord Jesus into heaven. I feel this way because every promise in God's Word was confirmed that first Easter morning when the grave was proven no match for the living God. Every truth claim of Jesus was confirmed when he rose from the dead and did what no person other than Almighty God can do... conquer death! The One who said He would rise did so, and Luke says He gave many proofs during that forty day period proving that fact and speaking about the Kingdom of God.

I wonder if Jesus reiterated some points He'd taught before to His disciples. Perhaps during the forty day period He looked at them through resurrected eyes and said, "I told you, let not your heart be troubled. You believe in God; you also believe in me. Can you believe that now? In my Father's house are many mansions. If it were not so, I would have told you. Do you believe that now? I go to prepare a place for you, and if I go to prepare a place for you, I will come again to take you to be with me, that where I am, you may also be. Will you believe that now? Seriously, I'm the living God. The empty tomb validates every promise I gave. You must believe what I am telling you now!"

The Gospel is a message of life and great expectation. The Kingdom of the Lord Jesus Christ is eternal life where our greatest expectations will be far surpassed. It's what Peter says in 1 Peter 1:3-4, "Blessed be the God and Father of our Lord Jesus Christ! According to His great mercy, He has caused us to be born again to a living hope through the resurrection of Jesus Christ from the dead, to an inheritance that is imperishable, undefiled, and unfading, kept in heaven for you." Can you see the message of the Gospel embedded deep within these verses? Like Matthew 6:33, they call us to the pursuit of God and the abandonment of that which is inconsequential. When we really believe the Kingdom of Jesus is worth everything, we seek after it and long for it, because it's a Kingdom of great expectations; it's a Kingdom of life.

You want to see the dichotomy between life and death, the Kingdom of Jesus versus the kingdoms of this world, vividly illustrated? Would you like to see the difference between great expectation from the Gospel and no expectation whatsoever? Let me tell you about two different funerals I've officiated.

The first funeral was that of Marion D. held in Southeast Texas. As far as any person knew, including family, Marion never placed his faith in Jesus for salvation. He never sought the Kingdom of God and His righteousness. Instead, he chose to live daily for himself. Marion may have been a friend to many, but selfishness and pride had been the flag he'd chosen to fly his entire adult life. On the day of his funeral there were only six people present, one of those being myself. As the son stood by his father's casket, he put a pack of cigarettes in his pocket and played Hank Williams' tune *Ramblin Man* on the portable radio. There was no peace, only tears of lostness that flowed that day.

If asked, Marion might have said that he believed in the historic Jesus, but he didn't believe the Gospel. Perhaps Martyn Lloyd-Jones summed up the religious beliefs of Marion best in this quote, "The trouble with the world today is not that people do not believe in the Lord Jesus Christ; it is that they do not believe in God."[11] Marion never embraced Jesus as God. His daily life denied the God who sent Jesus to this earth. So when we stood by the grave that day, a blanket of darkness and oppression hung about. The smell of death was in the air. There was no hope. There was nothing but the finality of death, the grave, and from all outward appearances, a Christless eternity.

In total contrast, I recently presided over the funeral of my uncle, James Spurlock. This man had been a devoted Jesus follower all his adult life. He'd raised his children to love God and love people. He had a practical faith that penetrated his entire life. He was the real deal.

When we walked into the funeral home, there were sweet tears of sentimentality due to the void this man's passing left in our lives. But there was no smothering feeling of finality and fear of the grave. It was supreme joy and happiness because we know he has passed from this life into the next with God. The great expectations he has held for decades were realized the moment his heart beat its last and he stepped into eternity. In the twinkling of an eye he was finally beholding everything he'd believed in by faith.

---

11  Lloyd-Jones, 211.

The joy and happiness we have was powerful because we know his life has continued in Heaven.

When comparing these two opposing illustrations, what are you expecting in your life? One is for the person who is lost and doesn't know Jesus Christ and has not answered the call of the Gospel. The other is for the person who has received Christ as Lord and Savior, believing the Gospel message. As a result of that, their eternity is infinitely better, because where they go is to a Kingdom of life and great expectation.

Where will you go when you breathe your last? I ask this that in all seriousness. If you've confessed Jesus Christ as Lord and Savior, the Holy Spirit will affirm your decision. There need not be a check in your spirit, or a moment of hesitation. God does not deal in spiritual confusion. He desires you to know precisely where you will spend eternity. You will either be buried in a dark hopeless grave to be resurrected to stand in judgment before God before being cast into Hell, or you have the promise of the Kingdom of Heaven awaiting you. Which is your destiny?

You must believe there is something lying beyond the veil into eternity through which now you can only see by faith. You must believe the Gospel message. Do you?

I realize what I've just shared is a stumbling block for some. There will always be those who have no spiritual ears to hear and are blind to the things of God. There will always be those whose hearts are calloused to the call of God and who reject the Gospel.

The Gospel of Jesus Christ is a simple message that can be embraced by a child. It is also vastly complex so that minds sharpened by decades of theological study cannot exhaust its depths. We will not understand everything regarding the Gospel until we get to Heaven. So now we believe by faith that what God said is true and we act upon what we believe accordingly.

Even those who heard the resurrected Jesus speak of the Kingdom of God asked Him in verse six, "Lord, will you at this time restore the Kingdom to Israel?'" Isn't that amazing? They're in the presence of resurrected Jesus, and they still didn't get it because it didn't click for them. Not that they didn't believe in Jesus, but they didn't understand about the Kingdom.

In other words, they were still thinking the Kingdom would be run by Israeli military and have a specific geographic location. What they really wanted to know is how Jesus would now deal with those pesky and oppressive Romans. Would they be kicked out of Israel now that Jesus, the resurrected Messiah had come to reign? Jesus' response went something like this, "Sorry, Charlie. It's not going to work that way. I have a better plan." Jesus always has a better plan.

The Kingdom of Jesus exists on earth today as a spiritual Kingdom. During the millennial Kingdom it will exist as a physical Kingdom. It will find ultimate fulfillment as both a spiritual and physical Kingdom in eternity. So to think that the Kingdom of the Lord Jesus Christ, at this time on planet Earth, is geographically located somewhere is false. You cannot look at a globe and find the Kingdom of God delineated by squiggly boundary lines. However, as you lift the globe looking for it, knowing there are more than seven billion people populating the surface, you may want to remember Psalm 24:1 that says, "The earth is the LORD's and the fullness thereof, the world and those who dwell therein."

Some are so frightened by the Middle East today that they may respond with, "Oh no, no, no. In *America*, we're the Kingdom of Jesus, and in the *Middle East*, they're the Kingdom of Satan." That is inaccurate and unbiblical!

The Kingdom of God means the reign and the rule of God in the lives of his followers *now*. It is a Kingdom that exists *now*. If you're waiting for the Kingdom of Jesus to arrive one day, correct your theology because the Kingdom of the Lord Jesus Christ is here *now*. It is the reign and rule of Almighty God in the lives of his followers *now*.

There is coming a day where Jesus' Kingdom will be a physical one. At the Second Coming, the Lord Jesus will return and will establish His earthly Kingdom at that time. Once established, He will reign for a thousand years on this earth. It is going to be a literal, physical Kingdom, but right now it's a spiritual Kingdom.

What is the challenge we hold today regarding the Gospel?

# The Spreading Flame of Christianity

If you study history, you may correctly assume that at times we were more spiritually-minded than we are in the twenty-first century. In fact, I've had people seek to convince me that we are living in a post-Christian era today. Just think about what is being said in those words before uttering something so foolish. That simple phrase dismisses the Gospel, denying the power of God unto salvation. It promotes an attitude that hinders spiritual awakening. In fact, it is the same attitude the religious leaders must have had when they stood at the foot of the cross demanding Jesus come down if He really were the Son of God. I've often imagined the High Priest and Jewish leaders patting themselves on the back for a job well done as they walked back from the crucifixion site. I can hear them saying, "That's that! He didn't come down from the cross. This controversy over Jesus is finished! Good job men." They thought they were in a post-Jesus era for sure but they were sorely mistaken.

The Gospel message is an eternal message that originated with God and will end with God. It will not be defeated on this earth. It is from God, empowered by God, kept by God. When we get to Heaven, we'll worship and praise God for His glorious Gospel for all eternity. But at this time, there is work to do. We are God's chosen instruments to spread the Gospel around this globe.

In verse 8, Jesus gives His call to go to work as His witnesses. He says, "But you will receive power when the Holy Spirit has come upon you, and you will be my witnesses in Jerusalem and in all Judea and Samaria, and to the end of the Earth."

As I write this, the government of the United States of America has shut down due to an inability to balance the nations' budget. Terrorism around the world is at an all-time high. Crime is thriving; murder rates are holding their own. The news on Wall Street is anybody's guess. Cancer and other inoperable diseases are taking their toll. Our military has been engaged in the Afghan war for years and there is talk at this moment about launching missiles at Syria because they used poisonous gas on their people. By any estimation, it could be said that evil is on the rise while the influence of the Church is in decline. But I'm not worried for one simple reason: the power of the Gospel of Jesus Christ!

Only God can guide us through the maze of problems confronting us. Only He can repair the breaches in the walls of righteousness that abound. God is our only hope. I do not know what tomorrow will bring but I do know this: Let all hell break loose. Let the devil rage on as he might, but he cannot change the ultimate outcome by destroying the power of the Gospel. The Kingdom of God is a thriving Kingdom, a victorious Kingdom. We will not be defeated regardless of the outward signs indicating our doom. The

Christian Church was founded on the blood of Jesus Christ, rises on the testimony of the Gospel message, and stands boldly through the power of the Holy Spirit. We will not be wiped out! We are overcomers because of the Gospel and the Gospel will continue to bring Kingdom growth until time is no more.

For now, let's remember the words of Paul in Ephesians 6:10-13, "Finally, be strong in the Lord and in the strength of His might. Put on the whole armor of God, that you may be able to stand against the schemes of the devil. For we do not wrestle against flesh and blood, but against the rulers, against the authorities, against the cosmic powers over this present darkness, against the spiritual forces of evil in the heavenly places. Therefore take up the whole armor of God, that you may be able to withstand in the evil day, and having done all, to stand firm." We have the power of Almighty God working for us; we simply need to continue advancing, refusing to give ground to the evils of Satan. We do this by heeding Ephesians 6 and advancing like Acts 1:8 commands.

When I was small, my family lived in St. Louis, Missouri for a few years. I remember visiting the St. Louis Arch when I was a little boy. If you've never seen the Arch, it towers an incredible 630 feet into the air. When you travel to the top of the Arch, you might even feel it sway if the wind is heavy that day. As I've grown older, the Arch has intrigued me for historic reasons. It is considered the "Gateway to the West" because it is the departure point of the great Lewis and Clark expedition.

The Gospel is the gateway to the world. There are no limits on it, unless we set them. Jesus says we are to be witnesses to the Gospel on His behalf around the world, in "Jerusalem, Judea, Samaria, and the ends of the earth." It's like the spreading ripples on a pond going outward when a rock is thrown onto the calm surface. Or, better yet, it is like a spreading flame of Christianity as the darkness is penetrated by the light of the Gospel.

Maybe an event in my life can help us see the point more clearly. About 11 or 12 years ago, my family lived down a country road outside of the town where I pastored. The house was painted an awful color of green so it became affectionately known as the "green house." Although we would have preferred different paint, we loved living there because it was seated on twenty acres of land. There is a lot you can do on twenty acres of country living.

The previous owner had left a large pile of brush just outside our back yard. One Saturday I told my seven-year-old son that we were going to burn the brush pile because it was an eyesore. Besides, the brush pile sat atop a prime garden spot, and I wanted to plant a garden that spring. So without much more thought, I lit the match and the pile began to burn.

Man did it burn! It had been there some time and was quite dry. In just a couple minutes the flames were shooting high into the air as the entire pile became engulfed. For some reason it never registered to me that the pile would burn from the center outwards, spreading in every direction.

Have you ever heard the phrase "ring of fire"? With the brush completely consumed in flames, the fire began burning outwards in every direction because the pile had been encircled by knee-high brown grass. When the moment of terror struck me that we were in trouble, I told my son to go tell his mother to call the fire department. He goes running inside, and I'm fighting the fire for all I'm worth with my shovel but I can't put it out. I had no water to put on the fire, only a shovel to fight the spreading ring of terror.

About that time I look up and there is my wife standing on the back porch with the video camera filming my debacle, unable to grasp the severity of the situation. To this day I think there is something wrong with that picture. I'm breathless and fighting the spreading ring of fire, and she's telling me to smile so she can capture it on video.

As the fire ring expanded, I noticed it heading directly toward the propane gas tank. Talk about a sight that will rob you of all joy. I knew my efforts needed to go that direction so I let it burn elsewhere as I fought the fire rushing towards the potential explosion. About then I see two neighbors running across the yard headed my way with firefighting equipment in hand. The cooperative effort of all working together saved the day and the fire was extinguished.

What a vivid illustration of how the Gospel is supposed to move. Jesus said it was to progress from "Jerusalem, Judea, Samaria, to the ends of the earth" because He is establishing a Kingdom with a multi-cultural populace. It is an international Kingdom where, as Revelation 7:9-10 describes, "a great multitude that no one could number, from every nation, from all tribes and peoples and languages, standing before the throne and before the Lamb, clothed in white robes, with palm branches in their hand, and crying out in a loud voice, 'Salvation belongs to our God who sits on the throne, and to the Lamb!'"

One day your life will end on this earth. When it does, you will either experience the Kingdom of Jesus as described in Revelation 7 or you will be denied access because you pursued the kingdoms of this world with misplaced vigor. There is only one right response - Repent! Confess your sins to God, believe the Gospel of Jesus Christ, and establish Him as Lord of your entire life. By faith, stake your hope of eternity on that which God has promised in His Word. Then, and only then, will you be able to live the life Christ called you to live, and that is living for *Simply Jesus*!

# bibliography

Bainton, Roland H. *Here I Stand: A Life of Martin Luther.* Peabody, Massachusetts: Hendrickson Publishers, 1977.

Barnhouse, Donald Grey. "Man's Ruin: Romans 1:1-32." *Romans,* vol. 1. Grand Rapids, MI: Wm. B. Eerdmans Publishing Co., 1952.

Boa, Kenneth and William Kruidenier. "Romans." *Holman New Testament Commentary,* vol. 6, Max Anders, Gen. Ed. Nashville, TN: Broadman & Holman, 2000.

Boice, James Montgomery. "Justification by Faith." *Romans,* vol. 1. Grand Rapids, MI: Baker Book House, 2000.

Bright, Bill. *The Journey Home: Finishing with Joy.* Nashville, TN: Thomas Nelson Publishers, 2003.

Chandler, Matt and Jared Wilson. *The Explicit Gospel.* Wheaton, IL: Crossway, 2012.

Geiger, Eric and Michael Kelley and Philip Nation. *Transformational Discipleship: How People Really Grow.* Nashville, TN: Broadman & Holman, 2012.

Hughes, R. Kent. "Romans: Righteousness from Heaven." *Romans, Preaching the Word.* Wheaton, IL: Crossway, 1991.

Jeremiah, David. *Signs of Life*. Nashville, Tn: Thomas Nelson, 2007.

Lewis, C.S. *Mere Christianity*. Nashville, TN: Broadman & Holman, 1996.

Lloyd-Jones, D. Martyn. *The Kingdom of God*. Wheaton, IL: Crossway, 1992.

Lloyd-Jones, D. Martyn. "The Gospel of God: Exposition of Chapter 1" *Romans*. Carlisle, Pa: The Banner of Truth Trust, 1985.

MacArthur, John, Jr. "Romans 1-8." *The MacArthur New Testament Commentary*. Chicago, IL: Moody Bible Institute, 1991.

Morris, Leon. "The Epistle to the Romans." *The Pillar New Testament Commentary,* Carson, D.A, Gen. Ed. Grand Rapids, MI: Eerdmans Publishing, 1988.

Mounce, Robert H. "Romans." *The New American Commentary*, vol. 27. Nashville, TN: Broadman & Holman, 1995.

Packer, J.I. *Knowing God*. Downers Grove, IL: IVP Books, 1973.

Tozer, A.W. *The Knowledge of the Holy*. New York, NY: Harper Collins, 1961.

# about the author

Byron McWilliams is the lead pastor of First Baptist Church in Odessa, Texas. He serves as a trustee of the International Mission Board of the Southern Baptist Convention and is a two-term past president of the Southern Baptists of Texas Convention. A lifelong learner, Byron has earned an undergraduate and two advanced degrees. Before being called to ministry, he worked as an accountant for one of the largest oil companies in the world in Houston, Texas. He has been married to his high school sweetheart, Andi, for 31 years and they have three grown children. Byron and Andi make their home in West Texas.

CPSIA information can be obtained at www.ICGtesting.com
Printed in the USA
LVOW05s0202241213

366562LV00001BB/1/P